# Decorating with Fabric

# Decorating
# with
# Fabric

## by Alfred Allan Lewis

### Photographed by Helen Buttfield

GROSSET & DUNLAP
Publishers    New York

Library of Congress catalog card number: 73-15128
ISBN 0-448-01303-7
First printing

Printed in the United States of America

For Ralph Lutrin

# Contents

# Color Illustrations

## Other Illustrations

# Introduction

In THE PAST few years, a fabric revolution has taken place in the interior design field. It has completely altered our concept of what can be done with fabric to change the look of a room or piece of furniture. It began with a desire for more pattern and texture in modern rooms. This soon developed into a delight in trying pattern on pattern and texture against texture and, ultimately, a melange of all in an exhilarating burst of color and line.

Fabric has become the weapon with which we can attack the prefabricated and standardized design that is being foisted upon us by contemporary builders and furniture-makers. It is the first line of defense against the sterility of the newer construction materials. It gives expression to an innate need for warmth, individuality, and color.

The crafts of fine woodworking, carpentry, and finishing are rapidly disappearing from the contemporary scene. The things found in stores are almost always overpriced, machine cut and finished, and tasteless. These pieces bear the same relationship to good furniture as a scrambled egg does to a soufflé.

What is true of contemporary wooden furniture is even more true of things made of newer materials such as lucite, aluminum, stainless steel, glass, and the acrylic plastics. They have as much personal style as stamped out cookies.

What all modern furniture seems to need is color for animation, texture for warmth, and pattern for personality. In short, it needs fabric.

Pillows, upholstery, slipcovers, throws—these are the obvious ways in which fabric can enliven furniture. What about covering the whole thing with fabric? As you'll learn, it's possible, it's fun, and it's inexpensive.

Instead of buying some overpriced piece with the dual built-in obsolescence of style and utility, let's experiment with "fabric-cating" unpainted furniture, old furniture from the attic, and junk furniture from the thrift shop. As will be demonstrated, the investment is minimal and the results extraordinarily satisfying from both the crafter's and the decorator's point of view.

Furniture is just the first stage in the fabric revolution against the dreary, the conventional, and the monotonous in design and decor. With fabric, drawers and closets can be made decorative as well as functional; a television set can become a part of the color scheme of a room instead of being a blot on it; a telephone can come in any number of colors and patterns instead of only Ma Bell's six decorator shades; an old box spring can become an Oriental divan.

Do you have a room with bad walls and a decaying ceiling, or one with monotonous walls and ceiling typical of new cubicle construction? Fabric can change all of that. It can turn a plywood or cement floor into something that can rival the parquetry of Versailles.

This book is intended as a primer on the fabric revolution as demonstrated by the man who can be called its George Washington, Mr. Luis Perez. By following his easy, step-by-step instructions, you will find that you, too, can become a master craftsman in fabric.

# Luis Perez

*"I didn't believe there were still craftsmen of this quality. I didn't believe anybody was still capable of this kind of workmanship."*
—NORMAN NORELL

THIS ADMIRING COMMENT by the great American dress designer was prompted by the sight of the first patchwork floor ever created by Luis Perez; the scene was the home of the New York socialite, Mrs. Wyatt (Gloria Vanderbilt) Cooper. The patchwork floor is but one of the many fabric innovations of Luis Perez. Despite a craftsmanship that many say approaches genius, his name is only known to those who carefully read the credits under photographs in magazines like *Vogue, House and Garden,* and *Glamour*—and to the people who have been the grateful recipients of his craft.

Perez has done the fabric crafting in some of the most photographed rooms in America. His tented ceilings are considered to be among the finest in the world. He not only invented the patchwork floor, but the entire concept of the pieced fabric floor. He has covered furniture with gingham, leather, and old Oriental rugs. When it comes to working with materials, he has done everything from finding a way to line an elevator shaft (for Geraldine Stutz) to devising a method for covering walls with early American quilts (for the aforementioned Mrs. Cooper).

And he works all alone. He doesn't even like having his customers on the premises, let alone attempting to help. He arrives with his tools. They leave. When they return, the job is done. In the case of Mrs. Cooper, she left for the entire summer while he single-handedly in-stalled the quilt room in her town house. Of course, that is the part of the story that is not told when photographs of the room appear in books and magazines.

When asked why he doesn't use an assistant or any helpers, he shrugs, "It goes faster when I do it myself. Besides, as I work, I change a little here—a little there."

One of the astonishing things about Luis Perez is that this extraordinary craftsmanship was self-taught. Aside from the fact that the women in his family were handy at making their own clothes and, occasionally, re-covering a piece of furniture, there was nothing in his background to indicate the career that would be his later in life.

"When I was growing up, only girls were permitted near the sewing machine. If I had asked to be taught how to use one, my father would have been very, very upset. When I did learn how to operate a machine, it was by watching the mother of a friend of mine."

Luis laughs at the recollection. "At home, even watching would have been considered a crime worthy of corporal punishment."

Home was the small Puerto Rican city of Quebradillas, where Luis was born and spent his first nine years; the happy household included three other children. Several tragic events soon turned the note of joy to one of sadness. The loving mother died. The father, unable to cope with raising four active young-

1

sters, was forced to leave the children with obliging relatives.

Luis was sent to live with an aunt on Long Island. A naturally friendly, good-looking child, Luis was soon contending successfully with the double obstacle of an alien environment and a strange language. He recalls that those first years in the United States were neither difficult nor simple. As far as he is concerned, it was a childhood like any other.

He was Puerto Rican and it was a period of rising resentment against the innocent newcomers. It was then that he developed a private world in which his secret sense of beauty and latent creativity could serve as buffers against the small cruelties and indignities that, unfortunately, remain a part of alien life in America.

When he was ready to enter high school, it was considered the practical thing for Luis to pursue a commercial course. An academic or art education was considered impractical for a young man who would have to be concerned with making a living. Luis learned bookkeeping, typing, stenography, and business mathematics —skills which he seldom uses today. People wonder if he will ever bill them for the work he has done. When asked, he simply says, "Don't worry. I'll get around to it. I'm too busy right now."

The truth of the matter is that he gets so engrossed with the problems of his current work that he often forgets the business side of the previous job. Some of his regular clients find themselves in the strange position of having to force money upon Luis. It's almost as if he were reluctant to accept payment for executing work that has given him so much personal pleasure.

After graduation from high school, Luis went to work in the stockroom of the main store of the I. Miller and Company shoe chain, located on Fifth Avenue in Manhattan. The job was not even remotely his (or anybody else's) idea of an auspicious beginning for someone wishing to pursue a career in the business world. But it was to prove the beginning of something far more rewarding, something beyond any of his dreams in those days.

At the time, I. Miller was a very exciting place to be. A brilliant young woman named Geraldine Stutz had just been brought over from Condé Nast publications and given her first job in retailing as president of the chain. Two of Miss Stutz's special interests were fashion and promotion. Vital to both was the display department, headed by McKim Glazebrook; his in-store displays and windows could make a loafer look like the greatest stylistic innovation in footwear since Cinderella lost that slipper.

Whenever Glazebrook was busy putting in new displays, the stockroom was not large enough to hold Luis. He was where the installation was being made—watching, learning, absorbing, trying to be helpful. Did a bulb need to be replaced, a yardstick held, a ribbon cut— if the staff was too busy to do it, Luis was there shouting eagerly, "I can do it. Let me do it."

When an opening came up in the display department, somebody naturally suggested that they give the job to—"what's his name, you know, that nice 'Puerto Rican kid.' "

Glazebrook later recalled, "I can't remember ever specifically stopping to teach Luis anything. He'd just watch whoever was doing something and, before you knew it, he was doing the job at least as well and probably better."

Miss Stutz said, "It wasn't long before Luis was the crown jewel of the display department. You couldn't actually say that you could see any growth in his abilities. They were just there—from God knows where—a mature talent. With those magic hands, he could execute anything."

It was in the Miller display department that Luis found his true métier—working with fabrics. He began by covering the panels used as backdrops for the shoes, shirring and swirling lengths of material, making curtains, using fabrics to enhance the decorative motifs of a display. The others soon took it for granted that, if materials were to be used, Luis was the one to handle them. He was neater, faster, more efficient, and certainly more inventive than anyone else.

When Gerry Stutz left I. Miller to become president of Henri Bendel, the department store, she asked McKim Glazebrook to design a new look for the venerable and tradition-laden store. Glazebrook asked Luis to work with him on a free-lance basis.

The first thing they worked on was Glazebrook's idea for revolutionizing the look of the entire street-floor level of the store. He wanted to break completely with the clichéd and overdone big store concept. What he envisioned was something that had the feeling of a European marketplace—a street of shops.

"When it was finished," Miss Stutz recalled, "it created a sensation in the press. Everybody came in to look and ooh and aah. In the beginning, that's all they did. Not buy, just look. At first, it seemed to us that our street of shops was a street of flops. In a short time it caught on. And it was the start of something new. It was the first time that a department store had individual boutiques. Now they all have them. Luis was responsible for a lot of the individual fabric touches—lampshades, upholstery, walls. Some of his work is still here, as bright and crisp as ever, even after all this time."

While Luis was free-lancing at Bendel's, he was offered a job that was to change the entire course of his career. He owed his lucky break to the fact that a certain Gillis McGill Addison had a case of bad walls.

Her husband, Bruce, and she had just taken a new apartment with a great living room encased in a set of walls that cracked, chipped, buckled, and generally resembled an aerial view of a Greek ruin.

She showed the room to her friend, the world-renowned decorator Valerian Rhybar. He looked at the walls and said: "Darling, there's only one thing you can do with them." He paused significantly. "Cover them. Completely. Floor to ceiling. In fabric."

It was a lovely solution except for one small problem. In 1965 one would have been very hard put to find someone who executed fabric walls for less than a fee that would have been as ruinous financially as the walls were esthetically.

Gillis was not only one of the most famous fashion models of her day, but, being one of those blessed with brains as well as beauty, had started her own model agency, Mannequins, Inc., which had offices in the Bendel building. She asked Joel Shumacher, of the store's display department, if he knew of anyone who could do her walls. Shumacher quickly replied, "Luis Perez. If it has anything to do with fabric, Luis' your man."

She called Luis and asked if he would be interested in doing the job. Luis replied, "I've never done anything like it before—but I guess I could. I'll try."

The fabric could not be applied directly to the walls because all of the imperfections would show through. The walls had to be padded first and the fabric hung over the padding with a staple gun. The problem was that one could not staple directly into the plaster. It would not hold.

Thin wooden slats were the solution. Luis framed the entire room with them, tacking them up along the ceiling, floor, corners, as well as around windows and doors. These thin slats gave him something that his staples could grip.

For the padding, which would give a feeling of opulence as well as camouflage the defects in the wall, he sewed together lengths of white flannel until he had a piece long and wide enough to stretch from the floor to the ceiling and from one corner of the wall to the other.

Using Elmer's Glue (or any of the white glues recommended for use on fabric, wood, or plastic), Luis pasted one end of the fabric to one of the corner slats stretching from floor to ceiling. Luis stapled over the glue. The flannel was pulled tautly and glued to the slat at the opposite end. Staples were again applied over the glue.

He then went all around the wall stapling the flannel to the slats along the floor and ceiling. When doing this for oneself, it is important to remember to pull the fabric so taut that there are no wrinkles and, also, to be very generous with staples, letting them overlap so that there is no space between them.

The last step is to trim the excess flannel along corners, ceiling, and floor. Single-edged razor blades are used for this purpose—a great many of them—since the action of cutting into the wood and fabric dulls the edges rapidly, and they must be discarded as soon as there is any decline in cutting power.

In recesses, over and below windows, above doors, Luis found it easier to frame out these areas in slats and apply fabric separately, rather than as continuous parts of the larger walls.

After the flannel was applied, the blue fabric was put up over it in exactly the same way.

3

This is called "stretching the walls" for the obvious reason that one does so much stretching to make certain that there are no wrinkles or any sign of slackness. In doing this, the stretcher must also make certain that the grain of the fabric does not buckle or waver.

Stretching the perfectly simple solid fabric in the Addison living room was comparatively easy; Luis was later to discover that prints and heavily-ribbed fabrics were more difficult to work. With these, he had to be sure that there were no waves in the weave and that, in the piecing, the repeats were consistent. All lines and designs had to be matched as they would in a wall-papered wall. Another thing he found was that some fabrics gave a great deal when they were stretched, causing distortions in pattern unless he was very careful while stretching. It was a good idea to test stretch a small piece of the cloth so that allowances could be made when hanging it on a wall.

To finish the job on Gillis's room, Luis cov-

*Illus. 1*   Gillis and Bruce Addison Living room.

ered the rows of staples by gluing commercial braiding of the same color as the wall over them (see illus. 1); he was later to make his own cording and ribbon to cover the staples. (For detailed instructions on making ribbon, see illus. 32–36; for cording, see illus. 39–42.)

With that first room, Luis knew that he had found where he wanted to work—in the world of interior design. Word of his remarkable abilities with fabrics went the rounds of that small and much-publicized circle of fashion and decoration. It was not long before the talented interior design firm of Zajac and Callahan was using him on jobs that required skillful "fabric-cation." A typical example is the handsome room in the Dwight Hemmion summer home in Quoque (see color insert, fig. 11).

Luis was learning as he went along, finding his own shortcuts, his own methods, his own approaches to the unique problems and virtues of working with fabric. One of the things he discovered was how much more versatile it was than paper. He said, "From the beginning, for me, paper was boring. It does not lend itself to use on objects or furniture. Even on walls, and in closets and drawers, it does not wear as well or look as rich. It tears easily. It cracks. When a client wants to change it, he/she can only paper over or remove it at great expense to paint over. With fabric, if you want to change a room even a child can remove the staples in no time. And it's gone. Finished. You are ready for whatever you want to do next."

As a fabric craftsman, Luis Perez did not really come into his own until he started working with two remarkable young women. Mica Ertegun and Chessy Rayner are partners in the interior design firm Mac II. Individually, they have that special brand of style that places them among the smartest women in New York City. As a team, their knowing combination of daring and good taste has made theirs one of the most successful decorating firms in the city.

From the beginning, Mica, Chessy, and Luis had a deep rapport. The women had no more than to tell Luis the effect they were seeking for him to find a way to be able to realize it for them.

Mrs. Ertegun has said, "It was more than only doing what we wanted Luis to do. He had his own sense of taste that blended with ours. He could take one of our ideas and extend it, enlarge upon it, take it a step further than we'd envisioned without distorting it or losing sight of what we were after. He has always had a sensitivity to fabric that comes from his love of working in it."

Luis Perez has done some of his best work for Mac II. It was while working on some rooms in Mrs. Ertegun's country house that she and he collaborated on the invention of the fabric floor. She thought that it would be very handsome to cover the floor with the same fabric used on the walls of one of the rooms.

The problem posed for Luis was how to make it durable and easy to clean. After some trial and error, he discovered that the way to do it was to stretch the fabric across the floor and paste it down. When the floor was completely covered with fabric, two coats of shellac and six of varnish were applied. The result was a fabric floor as hard as wood, one that could be swept or cleaned with a damp mop (see color insert, fig. 4).

Gloria Vanderbilt Cooper's well-known fabric rooms and floors were inspired by those she saw in Mrs. Ertegun's house (see color insert, fig. 2). The first and many of the subsequent ones, including the famous patchwork room, were done completely by Luis Perez.

Patchwork rooms are certainly not to everybody's taste, but the use of fabric in one way or another is an essential in modern décor and living. There are so many things that can be done with it to enliven the home. It might be something as simple as lining a drawer or closet, or as grand as putting up a tented ceiling or doing a pieced fabric floor.

The uses of fabric are abundant, and certainly no one knows more about them than Luis Perez. He has mastered all of the skills and secrets that make working with materials a pleasure. He also knows the many little tricks that save time and avoid problems. In the following pages, he will teach his craft and share his knowledge with the reader.

Before starting a "fabric-cation" job, it would be advisable to study all of the craft illustrations in the book. There are hints scattered throughout them that will prove very helpful.

# The Gingham Room

THE FIRST TIME that Luis Perez saw the non-descript room, it was obvious that he was seeing something that nobody else had seen. He looked around and said: "It has great possibilities."

The only reply that came to mind was, "As what?" But it was not voiced. It was better to let Luis continue without any sarcastic retorts.

"Let's have fun," he said to me enthusiastically. "Let's do a fabric room. I mean . . . a *total* fabric room. No sign of wood, plastic, metal, or paper. Just fabric."

Why not? The best way to demonstrate the marvelous possibilities of decorating with fabric would be to do an entire room in them—from floor to ceiling, table to telephone, closet to chair.

Luis spent two weeks doing the job. He was shadowed all along the way by the photographer Helen Buttfield, her lights, and her cameras. As a result, this book contains a record of everything he did. It gives step-by-step instructions of how he covered every part of the room

and each object in it. (For completed room, *see* color insert, fig. 1.)

In its original state, the room would never have won any architectural or decorative praise (*see* illus. 2). It was in a house similar to many summer places, the sort of building that, like little Topsy, growed without any specific plan. It was originally a tiny shingled ranch house with small rooms, sharply raked ceilings, and bare wooden walls. Later, a two-story addition was built onto it and, most recently, the garage was turned into a kitchen and breakfast room.

Luis' project room was situated in the original ranch house. It had once been a small bedroom but no longer served any purpose. There were already sufficient guest rooms, unless one was inclined to run a small hotel for friends wanting weekends in the country. Things accumulated in it with neither design nor reason.

There were many structural drawbacks to the room. The ceiling sloped much too sharply. The quality of the wood used for the beams

*Illus. 2*

and walls was so poor that not even three coats of white paint could disguise the knotty imperfections. The closet door was no more than a series of slats braced together; and the closet itself was built directly over the cellar stairs. As a result, it had a platform about 18 inches high, and one of the walls angled so sharply that nothing could be hung in approximately one-third of its area.

It was the sort of room usually found in an attic or basement—waste space that one is forever planning to convert into a spare bedroom or sitting room. If you have one, why not do it in fabric? Incredible as it seems, it's not only more beautiful but also less expensive than pickled plywood.

Considering the amount of yardage necessary to do even a small room, the cost might appear to be prohibitive. But it's not true. In planning the fabric room, Luis Perez explained, "We'll use light and inexpensive materials—cheap cottons. Aside from anything else, they're easier to work with than the richer upholsterer's fabrics."

In selecting fabric for a room, for covering furniture, or for any of fabric's myriad decorative purposes, the first thing to keep in mind is the aim; the second is where the fabric is to be used; and the poor third is the fabric itself. One must not be seduced by design or texture. The most magnificent fabric in the world can be wrong if it is used in the wrong way, in the wrong place, or for the wrong reason. Fabric is marvelous, an indispensable part of modern décor. But it must never be forgotten that it is a means and not an end.

Before discussing the particular fabric selected for our room and why it was chosen, it should be noted that, for all its architectural lack of distinction, the room was not without its virtues. Double doors gave out onto a broad sun-filled deck. Large tubs of bright red geraniums bordered each side. There was a perfectly magnificent view of a small harbor with clear blue water, broken, in warm weather, by a fleet of sailboats. It was agreed that whatever material was finally selected would bring those crisp, clean colors of the vista into the house.

Several fabrics were tried. Solid colors were immediately ruled out. There might be some visual problems in placing a unicolor chair and table against a floor and wall of the same color and fabric. It would be like the old Army test to see if an inductee was faking bad sight to get out of the draft. He was placed in a white room with a single white hook, told to undress and then hang up his clothes. If he found the hook, he was a fraud. One did not want to put a vain guest who refused to wear glasses to the same test.

Patterns in tones of one color were also ruled out. Like the solids, they might do very well if one were only doing walls, a floor, or a piece of furniture, but when everything was to be covered, there was a certain monotony, a lack of excitement in them.

Large prints were vetoed because they tended to make a small room look smaller. Floral prints would not work in this area; they put one too much in mind of an elegant little powder room. Multicolored tiny prints were also wrong; they gave the illusion of spots before one's eyes. To repeat, any of these fabrics might have been perfect in another setting and for another job.

Red and blue gingham was ultimately chosen for the room. Not only was it a very inexpensive fabric, but the red, white, and blue colors were festive, bright, crisp, and even patriotic. They also echoed the strongest shades in the view.

Gingham is a wonderful material to work with for another reason. Since the sizes of the checks vary, it is possible to create a subtle variety within a dominant pattern theme. Luis Perez used three different gages of check for the fabric room: 1", ½", and ¼".

Several lessons came out of the search for the right fabric for the room. Before starting to apply material to anything, it might be wise to review them.

1. Do not choose a fabric that will overwhelm the area in which it is to be used.

2. In a very bright space, avoid fabrics with shocking or vibrant colors, or those with a sheen to their texture. They will cause a glare that is most unpleasant.

3. In dark places, dark colors will lose tone and subtlety. They will be much too somber.

4. If the fabric has a print, always buy more

than you think you will need. A good rule to follow is: the more elaborate the print, the more fabric will be needed. This is because there is always wastage in cutting and matching the repeats. The more intricate the system of repeats in a pattern, the more you will cut away in alignment. (Note: Don't worry too much about this and don't throw anything away. It can be used to cover boxes, frames, or to do a patchwork floor (*see* color insert, fig. 3).

5. Whenever possible, permanent press fabrics are to be avoided. That wrinkle-proof virtue in the laundry room is a nightmare when trying to fit it into corners or around edges.

If one has a room whose appearance would be enhanced by fabric, and if one is fortunate enough to know Luis Perez and can afford his services, he is the man for the job. He has a talent for looking at nondescript plaster and wood and seeing texture, design, and fabric. It's a great gift that's not all that difficult to acquire. All it takes is an open mind and a love of pattern and color.

Try it. Look at a floor, wall, or table and envision it covered in some fabric that you adore. If that seems too ambitious, start small with a desk drawer. The wood might be beginning to splinter. There are nicks, ink stains, and pencil smudges.

On a shelf somewhere, you probably have some fabric left over from drapes or a slipcover. If the vision of the drawer lined in that material doesn't immediately pop into your mind, take it out of the desk and spread the fabric over the bottom. No more nicks or stains. In their place there is a decorative entity that is not only attractive, but also interesting to anybody who should open the drawer. (For detailed instructions, *see* illus. 249–253.)

On a more ambitious level, let's examine a closet. Some people are meticulous about their closets. Things are hung up neatly in garment bags. They're almost like enormous filing cabinets of clothing. Every dress, suit, coat, and pair of shoes is in its place and easily accessible.

Others are, shall we say, more random about their closets. Things are just shoved in wherever there happens to be available space or hangers.

But no matter what, most closets are slightly gloomy places to be opened and closed as quickly as possible, giving no pleasure beyond utility. This need not be the case. There is no reason why a door that is opened several times a day each day of the year should not lead to an area as nicely decorated as the rest of the house. Attractive transformations can be effected with some colorful fabric and a staple gun. (For instructions on "fabric-cating" a closet, *see* illus. 47–80.)

In this book, we're going to apply the principle of the drawer and closet to every part of the room. To show how simple it is, we're starting with what might look as if it is terribly difficult: the fabric floor. As you will learn in the next chapter, it is a labor of love that is no harder to execute than it is to adore.

# The Gingham Floor

UNTIL THE ADVENT of the fabric floor, quite literally, the floor had been at the bottom of the decorative innovation scale. Nothing new or exciting had been done with it for years. A beautiful floor was impossible to achieve without an enormous initial investment for installation and, generally, a large later investment in laborious upkeep.

A bare floor made of wonderfully grained wood can do much to enhance almost any room, but it is very costly to put one down. For those fortunate enough to have one, the maintenance involves a large expenditure of tedium in waxing and buffing. After a while, for all their loveliness, they begin to look a little cold, and there is the expense of purchasing scatter rugs to give the room a sense of warmth.

Great handwoven Oriental and European rugs are magnificent to behold. They are works of art in themselves, often passing from generation to generation as precious heirlooms. Like all works of art, the cost of a new or used one is often prohibitive.

Wall-to-wall carpeting is warm and can be inexpensive. The vacuum cleaner and electric shampooer have made it relatively easy to clean, except for the occasional spilled food or drink stain that will not come out and the burn that is there forever. Once it is down, however, there is no taking it up for the summer or to have it sent out for deep cleaning. It also presents some decorative problems. Green might have been a great color for the room the year that the rug was laid. What happens three years later if one should want to slipcover the furniture or paint the walls in a color that is not harmonious with that green? You can't do it. It remains a grassy floor forever more.

Gorgeous ceramic tiles are expensive, limited in use, and, though easy to care for, are also there forever. Linoleum and asphalt tiles are usually rather dull and almost always a decorative and economic compromise except in hard-use areas like kitchens, baths, nurseries, and "rec" rooms, where their durability more than compensates for any design inadequacies.

This is not to imply that each of the conventional ways of "doing" a floor does not have a great deal in its favor. In many instances, they did and still do provide the best decorative solutions. Nevertheless, the fact remains that there are no methods without some drawbacks for the average person who simply wants the prettiest and easiest floor with the least possible upkeep. Obviously, there was and is a need for a floor that is, at once, inexpensive, beautiful, novel, and that takes little time and effort to clean.

The answer to that need is the fabric floor, which is the result of the joint creation of Mica Ertegun and Luis Perez. The idea, which was born in the imagination of Mrs. Ertegun, became a reality by virtue of the craft of Mr. Perez.

Mica Ertegun and her partner, Chessy Rayner, had often used unipattern rooms in the jobs they did for their interior design firm, Mac II (*see* color insert, fig. 10). These strikingly effective rooms utilized the same fabric on walls, draperies and upholstery.

It seemed a logical extension of the same decorative motif to want to use that pattern on the floors. To have a carpet specially woven in the design would have sent costs soaring into the stratosphere. To stencil and paint it on the floor would have meant a time-consuming and possibly unsuccessful attempt at mixing precisely the same colors that were in the fabric.

Using the same fabric was the logical solution. But there were many obstacles to overcome. Most fabrics were too delicate to stand up to the normal traffic through a room. Scuff marks, stains, and burns could never be eradicated.

Despite the difficulties, Mrs. Ertegun wanted very much to try a fabric floor. It would not have been fair to experiment on a client; and so

*Illus. 3*

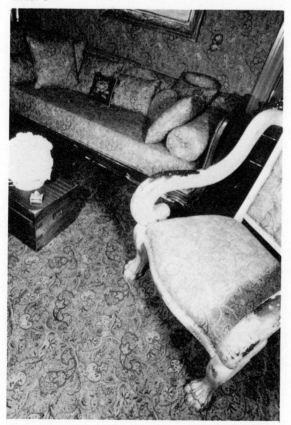

the first attempt at doing the innovative floor was to be made in a room in her country home in Southampton. The material selected was a handsome paisley dress fabric, but the mechanics of laying it were still to be devised.

Luis Perez had already demonstrated his phenomenal inventiveness and sensitivity in working with fabrics on several previous jobs for Mac II. When Mrs. Ertegun explained what she was after, Luis met the challenge with enthusiasm. He experimented with samples of the fabric glued to strips of wood until he came up with a way of laying a fabric floor that was as durable and easy to clean as linoleum and far more striking to behold (*see* color insert, fig. 2).

Another striking fabric floor (*see* illus. 3) is in the study of the New York apartment of Mr. and Mrs. Herbert Bayard Swope (Mrs. Swope is Maggie Hayes, the prominent jewelry designer and actress).

## Laying a Floor in a Single Fabric

*Tools:*

Large and small pairs of very sharp scissors.
About two dozen single-edge razor blades.
A yardstick (preferably metal) or similar straightedge.
A goodly quantity of white household glue (Sorbol or Elmer's both do nicely).
A large and small paintbrush.
A small paint roller and rolling tray.
Shellac ⎫
Varnish ⎬ or polyurethane

Before starting to lay the fabric, have the floor sanded or coat the entire surface with flat white paint.

1. Measure the floor to find out how much yardage will be necessary to cover it. Buy an extra yard or two. There will be some wastage.

2. Buy the fabric in one continuous piece. If possible, buy it still rolled on the cardboard cylinder on which it was shipped from the mill. If this is not possible, roll the fabric, rear side out, on a strip of 2″ by 2″ or on heavy cardboard the same length as the width of the material.

11

3. Use the suction tube of a vacuum cleaner (minus the brush) or a sturdy bristle broom to clean the floor of all dust, threads, splints, etc. You must start with an absolutely clean floor.

4. Pour some of the glue into the rolling pan; using the roller, apply it to an area of 15″ by the width of the fabric. Do this in the far corner of the room.

5. Unroll a little more than 15″ of the fabric and quickly press it to the floor face up. Leave the little extra bit of fabric lapped over the wall. Using your fingers, deftly smooth out all the air bubbles and work the material into the corner and right up to the edge of the floor. Work quickly and use a delicate touch. Try to keep the fabric as straight as possible to prevent the pattern from wavering. But do not pull too hard, or the fabric will stretch. (Since you will be working on your knees, have a pillow handy to rest them on.)

6. If the glue begins to dry before all of the fabric adheres, apply a little more with the roller. If it dries in the corner or along the edge, making it difficult to use a roller, apply the extra glue with the small paintbrush.

7. Using the single-edge blade, cut away the little lip of excess fabric at the far wall. Be careful to cut exactly into the angle between wall and floor.

8. Continue in this fashion, 15″ at a time, until you reach the near wall. Cut the fabric with the blade at the angle between wall and floor. If the edge of the blade is getting dull, change blades. If there is a door jamb, cut around it.

9. After every cut, clean up stray threads with a vacuum cleaner or broom. If there is any unravelling, use the brush to dab a little glue on the threads; this will stiffen them and make the threads easy to snip off with the small scissors after they have dried. Remember to clean up these little snips.

10. If there are any places where the wall juts into the room, press the fabric right against the wall angle and cut around it with the blade. If there are recesses, cut lengths of fabric sufficient to piece into them. Make sure that the repeats line up with the repeats in the adjacent column of fabric. Trim along wall angle with the blade. Before moving on to the next step, clean the floor; I cannot stress too strongly the need for a clean floor.

11. If the fabric has an edging with the mill's label on it, use the yardstick and blade to cut it off. Check for threads and get rid of them.

12. Go back to the far wall and start the second column of fabric just as if you were hanging wallpaper. Make certain the repeats line up with those of the first column. Then repeat the process of pasting down the fabric and checking for loose threads. When the glue thickens in the trough, add water to thin it.

13. When you reach the final column of fabric, you may need less than its full width. Simply cut into it along the wall-floor angle. Treat juts and recesses exactly as they were treated with the first column. When faced with permanent obstructions, such as radiator legs, cut and piece around them as you would if you were laying a carpet.

14. Go over the entire floor with the vacuum cleaner as a final check for loose threads and scraps of fabric.

15. As a final touch, you might outline the entire floor with cording made of the same fabric. (To make and apply cording, see illus. 73–76.)

16. Apply a coat of shellac over the entire floor, including the cording. Let it dry, then apply a second coat.

17. After the shellac has dried, apply six coats of varnish, allowing each to dry before applying the next. This may seem laborious, but the completed floor will possess a tough, resistant, long-lasting surface that can be cleaned with a damp or dry mop in a matter of seconds.

The application of a few coats of polyurethane has been suggested by some as an alternative to the shellac and varnish. In this writer's opinion, it does not work as well. Polyurethane is easily chipped and scratched. This not only spoils the look of the floor, but can also leave the fabric vulnerable to small rips, several of which will completely ruin the fabric floor. It can, however, be used in areas that are not subjected to hard wear. To apply polyurethane, put down coat after coat until a shine comes up on the floor.

## The Pieced Floor

Once Perez had mastered the fabric floor, he began to experiment by piecing together floors of several different fabrics. Although the work was more complicated, the basic principles were the same as those he had worked out for the single fabric floor. There were no additional tools necessary.

The esthetic pleasures that can be derived from the complex fabric floor more than compensate for the extra labor involved. Many of Luis Perez's favorite floors were inspired by early American pieced quilts. The gingham mock parquet floor in the fabric room (*see* color insert, fig. 4) is the same as the traditional Roman stripe pattern used in quilting.

The floor in the gingham room did not have to be whitewashed since it had already been sanded down. Luis decided that each block (of parquet or Roman stripe) would be a 12" square. To construct it, he used six gingham strips measuring 12" by 2". Of course, any fabrics that are right for the room can be substituted for the gingham. (To make a gingham mock-parquet fabric floor, *see* illus. 4–46.)

One last note on doing all floors. The shellac and varnish will dull the whites in most fabrics. Far from being a cause for alarm, I actually find it an extra source of joy. It gives the floor a patina that is extraordinarily handsome.

**The Gingham Room Floor**
*Illus. 4*
Measure the floor to locate its center and to calculate how many blocks of fabric will be necessary. Figure on one block per square foot. Starting at the center, mark the floor off in blocks until you have formed a rectangle or a perfect square. There should be no partial blocks in this floor. The space around the rectangle or square along the walls is treated separately as a border.

*Illus. 5*
Cut the fabric into strips measuring 12" by 2". Six strips will make one block. Gingham is easier to work with when the checks are uniform in size. To make a strip of gingham with 1" checks, count two down and twelve across. For nongeometric patterns, make a cardboard pattern piece measuring 12" by 2" and use it as a guide while cutting. When using gingham of several different size checks, precut strips of each type and keep them separate. Essential materials: scissors, straightedge (for measuring and cutting fabric strips), pot of white glue, 1" paintbrush, 3" paint roller and rolling pan, single-edged razor blades.

13

*Illus.* 6
Clean floor before pasting. Starting at the center of the floor, roll glue on floor for first strip.

*Illus.* 7
Apply first strip over the glue. Smooth it out so that there are no ripples, bubbles, or distortions. If more glue is necessary, apply it carefully under the fabric.

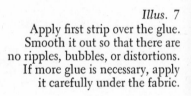

*Illus.* 8
Carefully lift any loose threads from edges and cut them away with a razor blade.

*Illus. 9*
Prepare for second strip by applying glue adjacent to the first strip.

*Illus. 10*
Continue in this fashion until the first block of six strips is complete.

*Illus. 11*
The completed first block, 1' square.

*Illus. 12*
Always remember to trim away
loose threads after gluing
each strip. If the glue thickens,
thin it by adding water.

*Illus. 13*
Start the second block directly
beside the first one and
perpendicular to it.

*Illus. 14*
Four completed blocks,
perpendicular to each other.

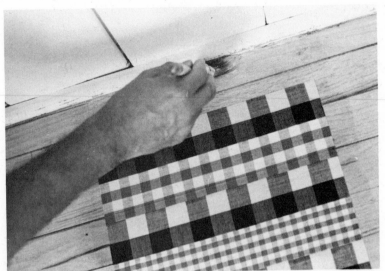

*Illus. 15*
When gluing next to wall, use paintbrush instead of the roller to apply glue.

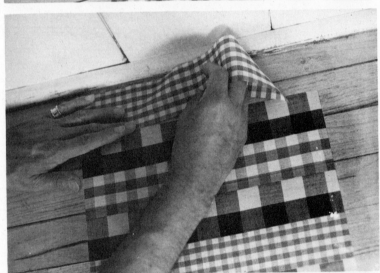

*Illus. 16*
Carefully glue the last piece of fabric at edge of wall.

*Illus. 17*
The nearly completed floor. Notice the border at the far end. (The adjacent sides of this floor were evenly divided into feet with no inches left over.)

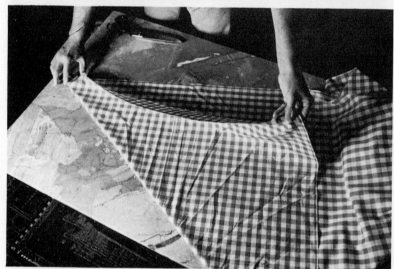

*Illus. 18*
The same border space was left at the opposite end. The borders are to be filled with a bias-cut strip of gingham.

*Illus. 19*
To make bias stripping, fold a length of fabric over to form a triangle.

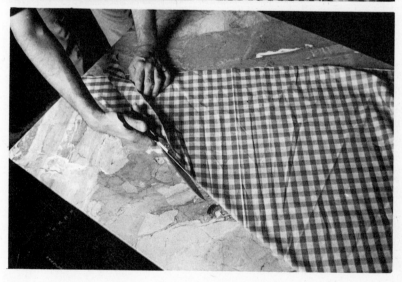

*Illus. 20*
Cut along the fold.

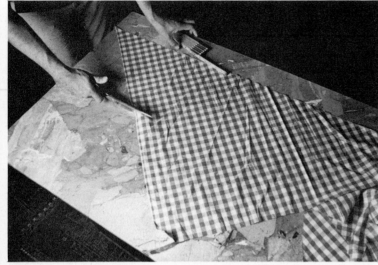

*Illus. 21*
Measure off the desired width of
the border on each triangular strip
and cut it off.

*Illus. 22*
Apply glue and paste down the
first bias-cut strip in the border area.

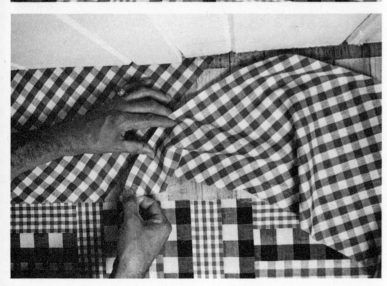

*Illus. 23*
Glue the second strip right next
to the first.

*Illus. 24*
Continue this process until the border is completely filled. Carefully match repeats; trim a bit of fabric, if necessary, so that the seams don't show.

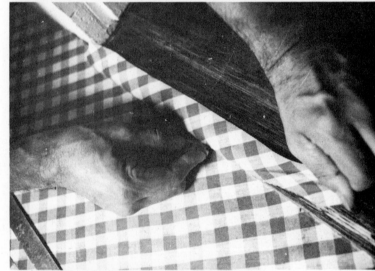

*Illus. 25*
Use a razor blade to trim excess fabric from the border along the door jamb.

*Illus. 26*
After lifting and cutting threads in border area with a razor blade, use the vacuum cleaner attachment to pick up any bits that still remain.

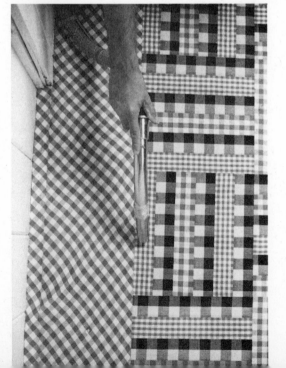

20

*Illus. 27*
Glue fabric over glass door jambs and trim with razor blade.

*Illus. 28*
For border with heat register, remove the grill, glue, and cover over with fabric.

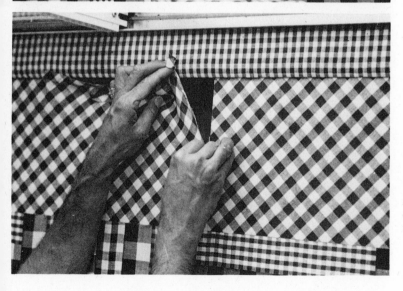

*Illus. 29*
After the glue has dried, feel the edges of the register with your fingers and cut around it.

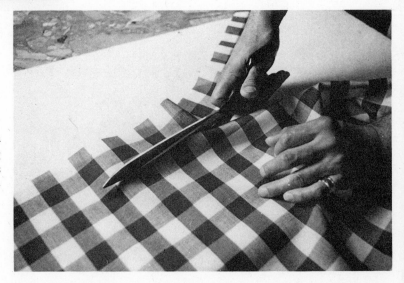

*Illus. 30*
The freed register, before the grill has been replaced.

*Illus. 31*
A corner of the room showing the border with pieced squares. A ribbon will be used to divide these squares.

**To Make Ribbon**
*Illus. 32*
Cut a strip of fabric three times the desired width.

22

*Illus. 33*
Keep cutting strips until a little more than the desired length has been cut. Glue the strips together, making sure that the pattern matches.

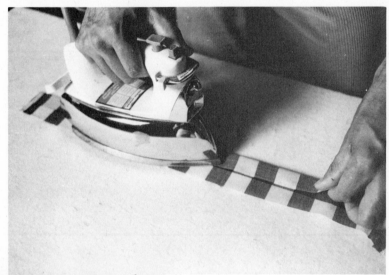

*Illus. 34*
Fold and iron one-third of the width of the strip over the middle third.

*Illus. 35*
Open the ironed flap, apply a thin stream of glue near the fold, and iron it sealed again. Repeat with the last third of the ribbon.

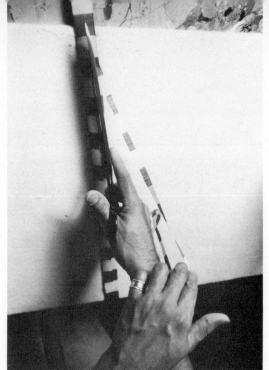

*Illus. 36*
Before the glue dries completely, cut away a
narrow strip from the last third of the ribbon so
that the edges are formed only by the folds.

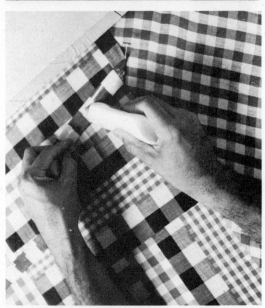

*Illus. 37*
Starting at one wall, apply glue to back of
ribbon and paste it down over the seam between
blocks and border. Continue to paste and
pin all the way to the opposite wall. The pins
will hold the ribbon in place while it is
drying; they should be removed after the
ribbon adheres completely.

*Illus. 38*
A view of the floor showing blocks, bias-cut
border, and dividing ribbon.
*The floor should have bias-cut cording running
around its perimeter.*

24

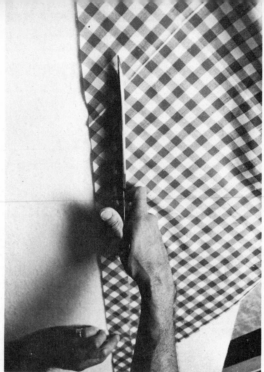

## To Make Cording

*Illus. 39*
Cut strips of fabric 1½″ wide
on the bias.

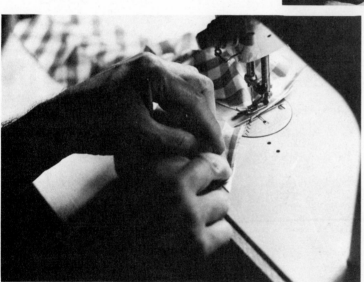

*Illus. 40*
Sew strips together on the bias to
make one long length.

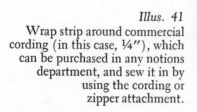

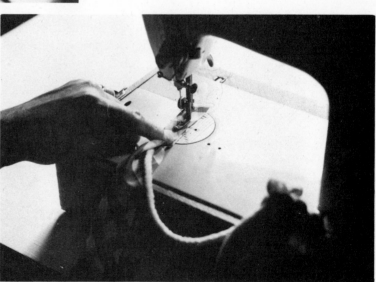

*Illus. 41*
Wrap strip around commercial
cording (in this case, ¼″), which
can be purchased in any notions
department, and sew it in by
using the cording or
zipper attachment.

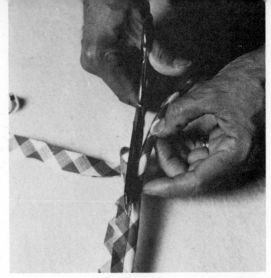

**Illus. 42**
After sewing, cut away excess fabric as close to the stitches as possible.

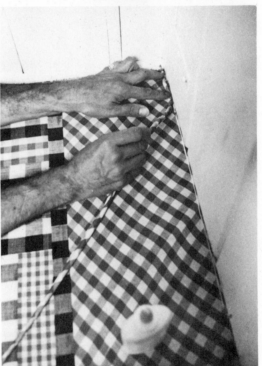

**Illus. 43**
Apply a thin stream of glue, a little at a time, along edge of floor. Press cording to it, seam side down. Continue around the room.

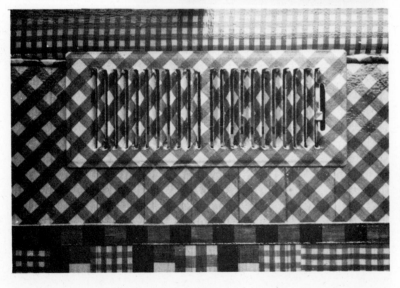

**Illus. 44**
If there is a register, cover it with the border fabric. Try to align it (as closely as possible) with the repeats (in this case, bias).

26

*Illus. 45*
Make a final search for stray
threads and snip them off. Vacuum.

*Illus. 46*
The finishing can be done in two
ways. Luis prefers to apply a
coat of shellac, letting it dry before
applying a second coat. For the
next three days, varnish is applied
first thing in the morning
and again at night. The other
method is simply to keep applying
coats of urethane until the floor
begins to take on a shine.

# The Closet

Fabric-cated Closet

IN MOST HOMES, closet doors are opened as often as the front door and yet the closet itself is rarely thought of in terms of decoration. The storage of clothes and linens may be done in the neatest and most orderly of fashion, but that is not enough to make an eye-catching and attractive area. There is no closet that will not be enhanced by some basic "fabric-cation." The simple application of some upholstery or drapery fabric can make the world of difference in its appearance.

Even the person who considers utility the only factor of importance where closets are concerned might stop and give additional thought to the appearance of the guest coat closet. This is one of the first things that a visitor sees when entering a home. With very little effort, it can be made into a charming prelude. Chances are that once the coat closet has been redone, the other closets will follow in short order.

The gingham room closet, with its awkward platform floor and one slanting wall over the basement steps, could not have presented a more difficult problem. But the outcome, as shown in the completed fabric-cation, (*see* illus. 76) could not have been more simple and delightful.

28

## The Closet

*Illus. 47*
The empty closet. Remove rack, shelves,
and braces. Precut the fabric so that
it is slightly larger than the section of wall
to be covered.

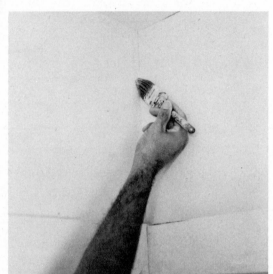

*Illus. 48*
Starting at the corner, brush on glue about
3″ at a time along the wall.

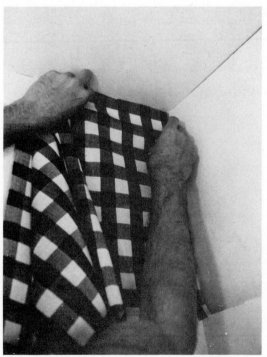

*Illus. 49*
Smooth and paste down a small portion
of the fabric. This must be done quickly to
prevent the glue from drying.

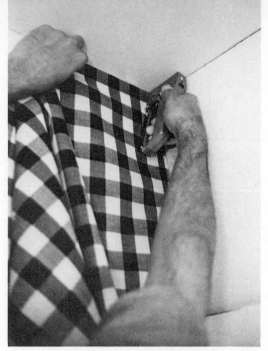

*Illus. 50*
Staple over the glued area along the top and corner angle. This is done to keep the fabric from shifting before the glue dries completely. The staples will be removed later.

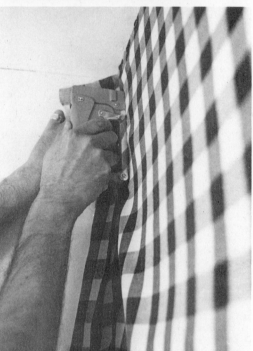

*Illus. 51*
Repeat steps in illus. 48–50, a few inches at a time, until you reach the end of the wall.

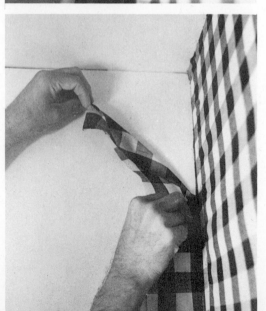

*Illus. 52*
Cut away any excess fabric at the corner with a razor blade.

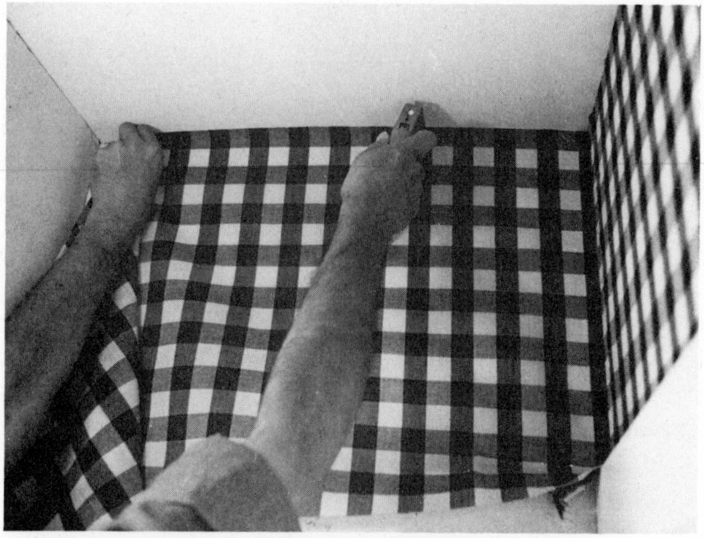

*Illus. 53*
Start the next wall, repeating steps
in illus. 48–52. Do this for all
the sections until the walls are
completely covered with fabric.

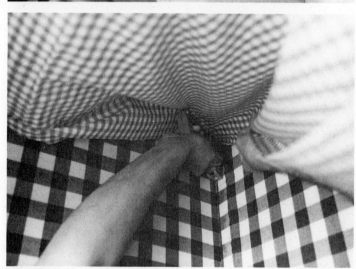

*Illus. 54*
Cut the fabric for the ceiling
and staple a corner of it in place.

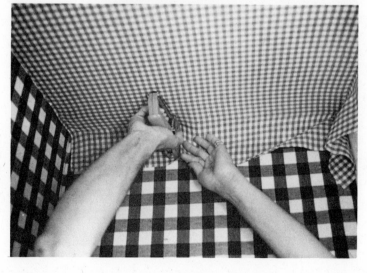

*Illus. 55*
Following the same procedure
used for doing a wall, apply the
fabric to the ceiling. Use finger
and palm to smooth out wrinkles
and bubbles. Trim excess fabric.

*Illus. 56*
A completed corner of the walls and ceiling.
After everything has dried, remove any staples
which may still be visible.

## Shelves and Braces
*Illus. 57*
Cut enough fabric to completely encircle the
shelf on both sides, plus enough on all
four ends for pasting. Paste
and staple to one edge.

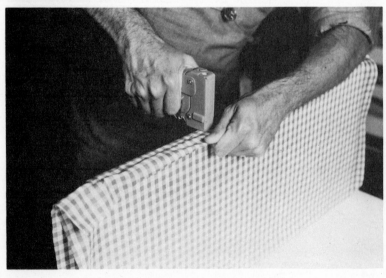

*Illus. 58*
Wrap and glue the fabric around the shelf.
Staple it closed. This double-staple edge will
face the wall and therefore not be seen.

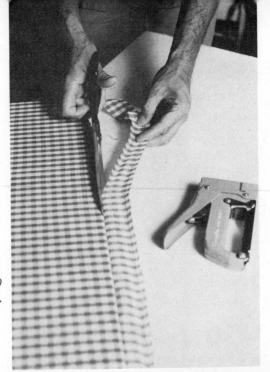

*Illus. 59*
Trim away excess fabric.

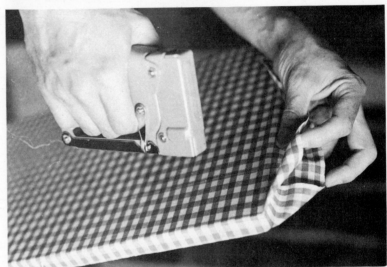

*Illus. 60*
Fold corners at short ends, just as if one
were wrapping a package.

*Illus. 61*
Staple underflap up and trim
away excess fabric.

*Illus. 62*
Staple overflap down and trim.

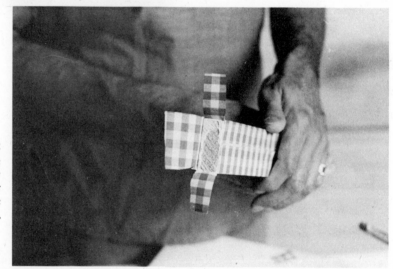

*Illus. 63*
For braces (or brackets), glue
and staple material completely
around object, as one did for
the shelves; instead of folding like
a package, cut slits at corners.

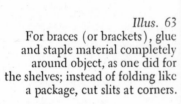

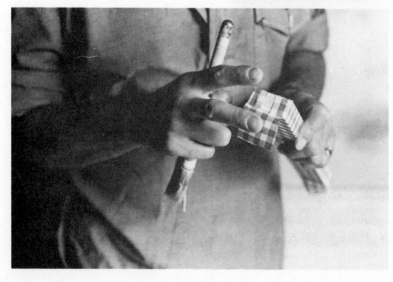

*Illus. 64*
Glue down slit flaps and trim.

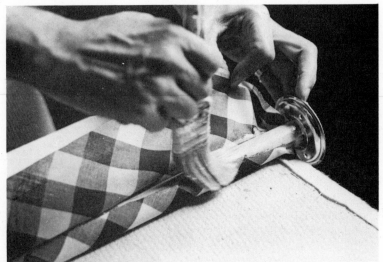

**Coat Rack**
*Illus. 65*
Cut enough bias-cut fabric
to encircle the rack.

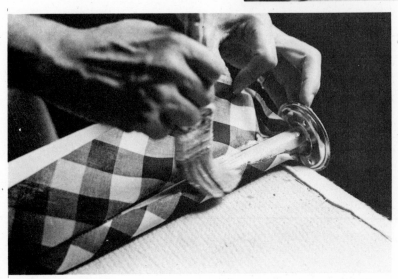

*Illus. 66*
Glue, roll, and smooth down
the fabric until the rack is
completely covered. If more glue
is necessary to seal it, add some
with a brush. Trim excess
fabric at ends.

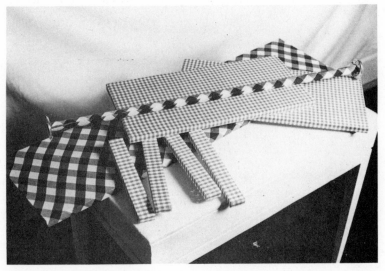

*Illus. 67*
The completed shelves, braces,
and rack for the closet.

*Illus. 68*
Rehang the rack and coat one
end with glue.

*Illus. 69*
Cut a slit in a piece of fabric
and glue it around.

*Illus. 70*
Trim excess fabric. Add more glue, if
necessary, to seal it. Repeat steps in
illus. 68–70 for the other end.

36

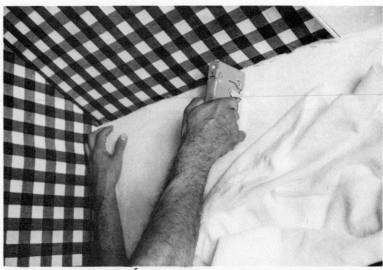

*Illus. 71*
For a luxurious padded floor, cut, glue, staple, and trim a lining of white flannel.

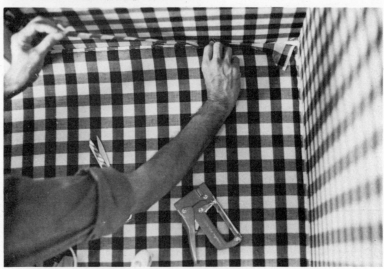

*Illus. 72*
Repeat step in illus. 71 with fabric. (Note: It is possible to do the floor without the flannel lining. If the latter method is selected, the floor must first be painted white or sanded down.)

*Illus. 73*
The completed floor, with handmade ribbon and cording trim.

37

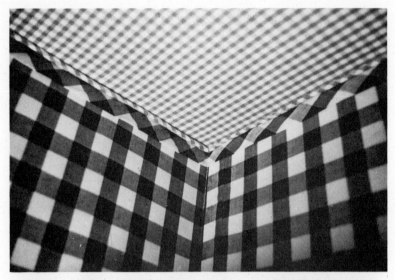

*Illus. 74*
Detail of ribbon and cording
at ceiling-level.

*Illus. 75*
Detail of finished cording and
ribbon trim around one
of the brackets and rack.

*Illus. 76*
The shelves, replaced
after covering.

*Illus. 77*
Remove the door from its
hinges and sand down (or plane)
the edges to compensate for the
bulk which the fabric will add.

*Illus. 78*
Cut, glue, and staple a lining
of white flannel. Make certain the
fabric is taut.
Trim excess flannel.

*Illus. 79*
Repeat with fabric. (Note:
if a good door is painted white,
there is no need for lining.
Fabric can simply be glued
directly onto the door.)

*Illus. 80*
Remove staples used to hold
fabric while the glue was drying.
(Note: For all gluing, personal
judgment is essential; based
upon available space, decide
whether to use a brush or roller.)

*Illus. 81*
Wyatt and Gloria Cooper Bedroom © 1970 *Van Nostrand Reinhold.*

40

# Other Fabric Floors

Luis Perez has recently been experimenting with the possibilities of crocheted and lace floors (*see* illus. 82). By the time this is read, he will undoubtedly have done just such a floor for some client who also recognizes the handsome prospects of such a floor.

Once the technique is mastered, there is no end to the things that can be done with a fabric floor. If you want the look of Oriental carpets, why not apply to the floor the sort of fabric used on the walls of Mr. and Mrs. William Rayner's sitting room? (*See* color insert, fig. 12.) They can either be treated as a giant carpet in a very large panel or in area rug fashion, scattered over a painted or single fabric floor.

There is no reason why one cannot have a modern art floor. What could be simpler than to trace a painting by Frank Stella, Jasper Johns, or Andy Warhol in fabric and apply it to the floor? On the scale of more important art, Picasso and Miro designs are available in fabric. They would make wonderful and important floors.

Why not a découpage floor for a Victorian room? All that need be done is to follow the principles of découpage, using fabrics instead of paper. Cut out flowers and figures from prints and paste them to the floor. Cover all or part of a surface that has previously been sanded or whitewashed. Check for threads and apply varnish and shellac. Don't worry about the ridges formed by overlapping pieces; they will become almost silken smooth under the coats of protectors. The resulting floor will have the enameled look of a découpage box and be much more durable.

Another exciting possibility would be to use the floor as a canvas and do a gigantic fabric collage. On this sort of floor, paper can be used. The shellac and varnish will protect it, but paper will never have the same textural interest as fabric.

## The Patchwork Floor

The patchwork floor is one of Luis Perez's most exciting achievements (*see* color insert,

fig. 3). It was conceived for Mr. and Mrs. Wyatt Cooper. Luis had previously covered the walls of their bedroom with old quilts. There were also to be patchwork drapes plus a spread. When it was suggested that conventional carpeting be used for the floor, Luis asked to be allowed to do a patchwork floor. To her vast credit, Mrs. Cooper agreed (*see* illus. 81).

Luis is a saver of scraps of material. Once you get into fabric, you will find this to be a very useful habit. Scraps can be used to cover boxes, frames, and also to make a patchwork floor. Mrs. Cooper's floor is covered with bits and pieces gathered from dozens of jobs for people like Geraldine Stutz, Gillis Addison, Mica Ertegun, Chessy Rayner, and Zajac and Callahan.

When the floor was finished, it was the perfect quilt island of pristine artistry to set off a room fashionably cluttered with Mrs. Cooper's collages and other *objets d'art.*

If a patchwork floor suits your fancy, it is very easy to create. (*See* illus. 83–89.)

41

## The Patchwork Floor
*Illus. 83*
Scraps and tools necessary to make a patchwork floor.

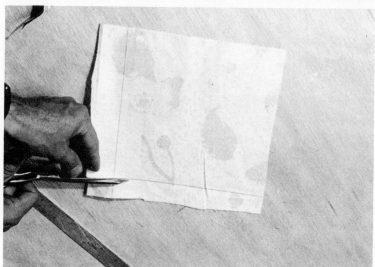

*Illus. 84*
Square off jagged edges of fabric and cut away along the ruled lines.

*Illus. 85*
Prepare corner of floor with glue. When glue thickens, thin it with water.

*Illus.* 86
Use brush to apply glue to small ribbonlike strips.

*Illus.* 87
If necessary, square off edges of some patches and cut away excess fabric with blade. Just how much is up to the crafter's individual sense of design. The two important things to avoid are overlapping of patches (they must abut without spilling over) and loose, frayed edges.

*Illus.* 88
The corner of the floor beginning to take shape.

*Illus.* 89
The floor as it appears before the application of shellac and varnish (or urethane), in the manner already described for the gingham room floor. Apply the same rules—searching for threads and vacuuming—to all fabric floors.

## The Appliqué Floor

Baby Jane Holzer was commissioned to decorate an extremely contemporary apartment for Mr. and Mrs. Kent Klineman. In contrast to the "with it" look of the rest of the rooms, they wanted a rather Victorian nursery. Mrs. Klineman had a collection of old quilts; the decorator thought it would be marvelous to use one for the floor.

As a Southamptonite, Mrs. Holzer knew Luis Perez's work from the rooms he had done there for Mica Ertegun, Chessy Rayner, and Gloria Cooper. She commissioned him to do the floor.

Luis loved the idea and set to work. The result was a wonderful bit of childlike fantasy (*see* color insert, fig. 5).

Using an old quilt top as a center, he built up the floor with gingham patchwork, ricrac, ribbon, and commercial appliqué pieces cut in the shape of baskets and the traditional Dresden plate motif. The first thing he did was to paste a huge rectangle of red gingham in the center of the room. He then glued the quilt cover over this rectangle. Around the area he used ribbon. The next border consisted of solid yellow alternating with the appliqué baskets glued on squares of printed fabric. This was followed by a solid edging outlined in ricrac and festooned with a large appliqué basket. The next section was comprised of gingham patchwork fancifully appliquéd with bits of colored ricrac. This was first followed by a line of solid fabric and ricrac and then by the border of Dresden plate appliqués. The area stretching from the plates to the wall was filled in with patchwork of various fabrics and ribbons. (*See* illus. 90.)

When everything was glued down, the shellac and varnish were applied. If there was ever any question of the strength of a fabric floor, this one would answer it. The Klineman children were and still are extremely active youngsters. The floor has been subjected to bicycle riding, roller-skating, blocks, and all manner of mechanical toys. Furniture is pulled across it daily as part of the children's fun and games. For all this super wear and tear, the floor re-

mains as handsome and lustrous today as it did on the day that Luis completed it.

Fabric floors for nurseries, bedrooms, dens, sitting rooms, in solids or patterns, in single fabrics or many fabrics—the results are always exciting. The actual process of putting one down is not difficult. A combination of hard work and patience is necessary, but once that is over there is a floor to give pleasure for years to come. The time and labor will be more than repaid in the time and labor saved in subsequent upkeep.

# The Gingham Ceiling

THE GINGHAM FABRIC room was intended to serve different functions during the different seasons. During the warmer summer months, the idea was to suggest a tented pavilion that would bring the outdoors into the house. In winter, it was meant to be a warm and cosy nook with cheerful colors to brighten the often gray and drear skies of the far eastern end of Long Island.

If fabric is going to be used on both ceiling and walls, it is usually best to start by doing the ceiling, especially if the walls are to be shirred. The reason is that the shirring will help to mask the rougher edges of a tented ceiling.

With a stretched fabric wall, one can start by doing the wall if a skirt is to be affixed to ends of the tent. Otherwise, it is best to do the ceiling first and then attach the framing slats over the edges of the tent so that they are tucked under the wall and masked by it.

Because the gingham room was to have shirred walls, the tent was hung first. A tented ceiling is a thing of beauty and can be a joy, if not forever, at least for a very long time. Although seemingly fragile, it has very real advantages and strengths when compared to the paint and plaster ceiling. For one thing, it will never crack or chip. It is also easier to clean. A vacuum cleaner will do the job very nicely. It certainly lasts longer, for it does not have to be refinished every two or three years. Another major advantage is that, in addition to the opu-lence it creates in any setting, it also hides flaws in a bad ceiling.

In the gingham room, the ceiling presented many problems. First of all, it had a severe rake, making one side of the room a good 14″ higher than the other, and giving the entire room a "lean-to" look. (Another plus for the tent is that it will lower or even a ceiling.)

This ceiling was not plastered over, and the painted planks were made of an undistinguish-able and knotty wood. The beams that sup-ported them were no more than 2″ by 4″, added neither grace nor charm, and were most assur-edly devoid of any sense of style (*see* illus. 91).

*Illus. 91*
The ceiling in its natural state.

Luis Perez felt that a tent would offer the best as well as one of the least expensive solutions. It would not only even the height of the ceiling; it would also cover the many defects in a very handsome fashion, thus adding greatly to the ultimate effects desired in the room.

A tented ceiling looks terribly complicated. Hanging it would appear to be a cumbersome problem involving several people. Actually, it is so simple that one person can install it by him- (or her-) self.

The tent is composed of four pie-shaped wedges radiating from the center of the room to each of the four walls and corners. (For one completed wedge, see illus. 121.)

In addition to the tools already listed for doing a floor, a staple gun and a goodly supply of staples are necessary.

## Estimating the Amount of Fabric Necessary to Make a Tented Ceiling

Measure the length of each of the four walls. Mark the exact center of the room. If there is a lighting fixture or chandelier which will remain in use after the tent is up, use it as the focal point even if it is slightly off-center.

Since the length of each wall will undoubtedly be several times the width of the fabric (and even that length will be at least doubled), the wedges are composed of panels of fabric that are sewn together. To determine how many panels will be necessary for each wedge, multiply the length of the wall it is to meet by two (more if a tent with very luxurious and close folds is desired) and divide the width of the fabric into that figure.

The length of the middle panels will be about 2″ longer than the distance from the center of the room to the wall that the particular wedge will meet. The two end panels (those that will meet the corners) are 18″ longer than the other panels.

To determine the amount of fabric one should buy, simply add up the length of all the panels in all four wedges.

Let us take the fabric room as an example. It measures 9 feet by 12 feet (or 108″ by 144″). The fabric had a 36″ width. There were six panels in the wedges for each of the shorter walls (36″ into 2 x 108″ or 216″). Four of the panels each measured 74″ (two inches more than the 72″ which represented the distance from the center of the room to the wall, or half the length of the longer wall). The two end panels measured 92″ (or 18″ longer than the inner panels). Totaling the panel lengths, one found that each of the shorter wall wedges needed 480″ (or 13 yards plus 1 foot of 36″ wide fabric).

When the calculations were completed for the longer walls, it was found that each of them required about the same amount of fabric as was necessary to make a wedge for the shorter wall; the explanation for this was simply that the shorter length of each panel compensated for the additional panels.

The fabric necessary for the tent came to 53 yards plus 1 foot of 36″ wide fabric. A full 54 yards of fabric was purchased. The extra 2 feet were used to make the rosette for the center of the ceiling.

(For detailed instructions showing exactly how the tented ceiling and the rosette were made and hung, see illus. 92–121. For a view of the completed ceiling, see color insert, fig. 6).

### The Tented Ceiling
*Illus.* 92
Find the center of the ceiling and tack up a small rectangle of plywood. If there is a lighting fixture that is to remain functional after tenting, take that as the center. Remove the fixture, cut a hole in the plywood for the wiring to come through, then tack up the rectangle.

### Making Rosette For Ceiling Without Fixture
*Illus.* 93
Bolt one of the flanges to the center of the plywood or, in the case of a lighting fixture, bolt it over the opening through which the wires pass. The wires must come through the flange. If the ceiling is flat and will sustain the flange without additional support, there is no need for the plywood. Simply bolt the flange directly to the center of the ceiling or over the fixture wires.

*Illus.* 94
The little pipe will eventually screw into the flange. In case of a light fixture, the wires will run through it.

*Illus. 95*
Cut a wooden disk (or have one cut by a lumber yard). Its size will vary according to the size of the room. In no case should it be smaller than 9″ in diameter. Bolt the other flange to it. The photograph shows the length of pipe being fitted into this second flange. If there is a fixture, a hole should be cut in the center of the disk to enable wires to come through the pipe, both flanges, and the fixture. After the tent is finished, this will make it possible to rehang the fixture.

*Illus. 96*
Cut another disk whose diameter is slightly more than one-third of the diameter of the larger disk. It should be large enough to cover the flange bolts.

*Illus. 97*
For the disks, cut two circles of white flannel, each about 4″ larger in diameter than the respective disk.

49

*Illus. 98*
Using a staple gun, cover the disks
with flannel. Start by pulling
the material tautly and placing
anchor staples on
four sides.

*Illus. 99*
Pulling the fabric tightly, continue
to staple all around the disks.
Overlap the staples; they're
inexpensive, so be very
generous with them.

*Illus. 100*
After covering, trim away the
excess fabric to within ½″
of the staples.

*Illus.* 101
Repeat steps in illus. 98–100 with gingham, using different colors and different check sizes for each disk.

*Illus.* 102
The disks covered in gingham.

**Making Shirred Cording Trim**

*Illus.* 103
Using 1″ wide cording, measure off and cut enough cording to circle both disks. Bind with thread at the beginning, end, and point where the cording will be cut into the lengths for both disks. Cut them.

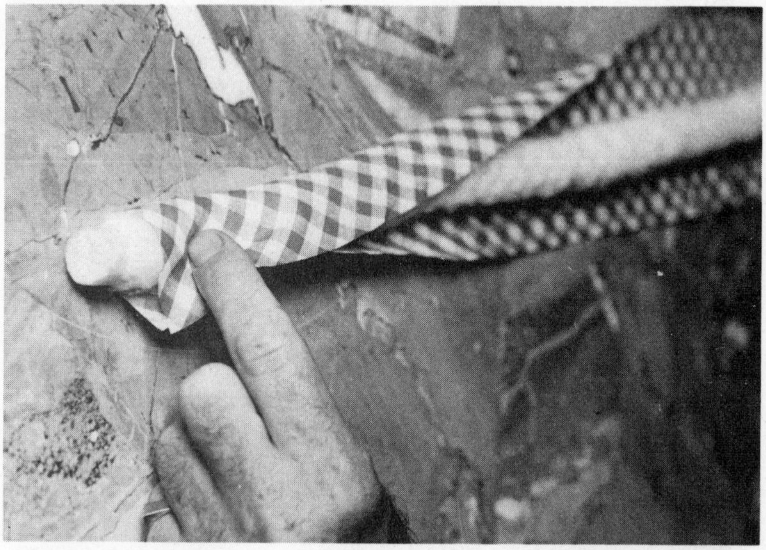

*Illus.* 104
Cut strips of gingham wide
enough to make jackets for the
pieces of cording; cut them
double in length.

*Illus.* 105
Using zipper or cording
attachment, make the jacket
(minus the cording).

*Illus.* 106
After completing the jacket, gather
it on a long pencil or stick and
turn it inside out.

*Illus. 107*
Tie the pencil to the end of the cording and push it through the jacket, pulling the fabric down over the cording.

*Illus. 108*
After shirring the fabric on the cording, sew one end up.

*Illus. 109*
After shirring both cords, glue them around their respective disks; hold them in place with pins until the glue dries. Press hard to make sure it adheres.

53

*Illus. 110*
As a last step, snip off extra cording above the thread binding and sew the ends of the shirred fabric together.

*Illus. 111*
The completed larger disk of the rosette.

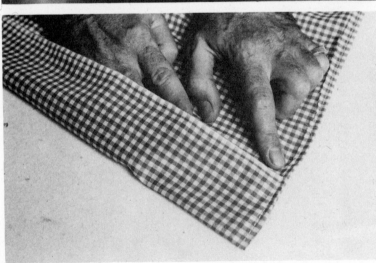

**The Tent Fabric**
*Illus. 112*
Figure out the amount of fabric needed for each wedge or wall. Sew together all of the fabric necessary to make one wedge. Fold up a 3″ edge at the shorter sides. Hold them in place by making a ¼″ hem running over them and across the top of the attached panels.

*Illus. 113*
Thread about 2′ of nylon tufting twine (knotted at the end) on a needle. Make 2″ folds in the fabric at the hemmed end. Sew them together with the twine just below the hem, midway in the folds.

*Illus. 114*
Attach the bottom part of the flange to the pipe and ceiling.

*Illus. 115*
Gather the folds on the twine and loop the latter around the pipe several times, being careful to pull in the gathers so that they do not show below the disk. Sew the thread back through the first stitch.

*Illus. 116*
The fabric for one wedge attached
to the disk.

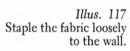

*Illus. 117*
Staple the fabric loosely
to the wall.

*Illus. 118*
Pull and staple tightly,
using many staples.

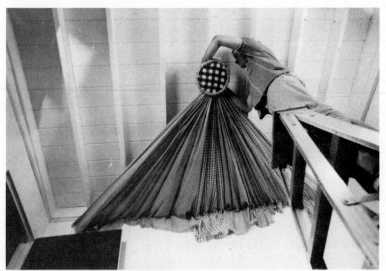

*Illus. 119*
If necessary, retie and tighten around the pipe to make the fabric really taut.

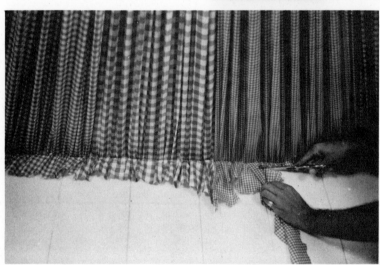

*Illus. 120*
Trim the excess fabric beneath the row of staples.

*Illus. 121*
The completed wedge. Repeat steps in illus. 112–121 with each of the other three wedges. There is no need to sew the four sections together. Simply make certain that the stapling is continuous all around the walls, with each successive wedge beginning at precisely the point where the previous one leaves off. The very last step is to attach the smaller disk by hammering through its sides into the larger disk at the point where the nails are obscured by the shirred cording.

# The Gingham Wall

THERE ARE TWO kinds of fabric walls. The stretched wall, which we have already discussed, has a formal elegance (*see* color insert, fig. 7). The shirred wall is soft and opulent (*see* color insert, fig. 8). Both enhance the appearance of any room and serve the useful function of covering bad walls. They are not only more durable than any type of paint, but are softer, more handsome, and easier to remove than wallpaper.

There were many reasons why the shirred wall was the type selected for the gingham fabric room. The primary one was esthetic. The soft folds would continue the feeling of tent or pavilion. Beyond that, the fabric-covered furniture would contain many stretched surfaces and hard lines that would benefit from the muting contributed by the looser treatment.

There was also the general feeling that rich and fabulous fabrics were dazzling when stretched, so that one could appreciate the full panoply of their texture and design. The modest gingham tended to be rather prosaic when stretched across a whole wall. It would need to be broken by a great many pictures, which would only create clutter in this setting.

The big drawback to a shirred wall is one of economics. It takes three times as much fabric as the stretched wall, which is another good reason for not using very expensive fabrics for this type of decoration, unless, of course, one is seeking an extraordinary elegance and considers price of no importance in the pursuit of it.

Gingham, inexpensive little cotton prints, the boldly patterned new bed sheets—all of these make wonderful fabrics for shirring. Heavier fabrics, moreover, are usually difficult to handle. Permanent press materials should be avoided, if possible, for they resist pleating and shirring with the same vigor with which they fight against wrinkling.

Shirring can be done on rods so that the wall can be taken down for laundering or dry cleaning. It is not the best method; rods are extremely difficult to hang and adjust along the walls of an entire room. Stapling is far easier for the home crafter who wants to do it alone.

There is actually very little reason for laundering or dry-cleaning a shirred wall. There is always the danger of shrinking (which can throw the line of the wall off) and fading (which can ruin the entire room, especially if the same fabric is used on furniture or for a tent). Using a vacuum cleaner once or twice a week should keep a shirred wall looking clean and bright.

The best way to do a shirred wall is with shirring tape, an item which can be purchased at most fabric and notions shops. It can be attached to the fabric very easily and is extremely simple to use.

In some rooms, a billowing, curtain-like effect is wonderful. This is achieved by using the shirring tape only along the top of the fabric. The bottom is hemmed and floats freely into the room. For this type of wall, it is important to add enough fabric to make that bottom hem.

For the fabric room, shirring tape was used on both the top and bottom of the material; both were stapled in place so that the shirred gingham clung to the walls. This method is preferable for a small room because the freely hanging folds tend to reduce the overall area.

To figure out the amount of fabric necessary for a shirred wall, divide the width of the fabric into three times the circumference of the room. This will give the number of panels necessary. Multiply it by a few inches more than the height of the room for the final result. An addition of 2″ is sufficient for a wall to be shirred on top and bottom, where only a slight turnup is necessary when the tape is applied. Add 4″ for the billowing wall so that there can be a healthy hem at the bottom.

Cut the required panels for each wall to a few inches more than the height of the room. Sew them together until you have one piece three times the length of the wall. Do this for each wall.

For the gingham room, the walls were done in red gingham with ¼″, ½″, and 1″ checks which were alternated in the piecing. One-third of the total fabric was purchased in each size.

Fabrics with more intricate patterns present no problems of wastage in being pieced for a shirred wall. One does not have to bother with matching repeats, for the seams are lost in the process of shirring.

For windows and doors, make separate shirred panels to be hung above and below them, as well as to cover the doors themselves.

(For instructions on doing a room with shirred walls, *see* illus. 122–148.)

**The Shirred Wall**

*Illus. 122*
After calculating the amount of fabric necessary and piecing together all of the panels for each wall or section, turn up a 1½″ hem and sew through the shirring tape. Do this both at the top and bottom. (If the wall is only to be shirred on top, simply hem the bottom and ignore all shirring instructions pertaining to the bottom.)

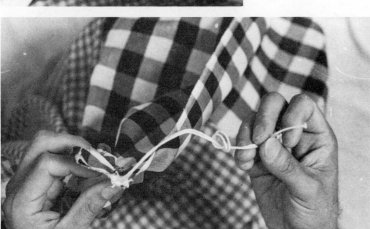

*Illus. 123*
Gently pull the two strings out of one end of the shirring tape and knot them.

59

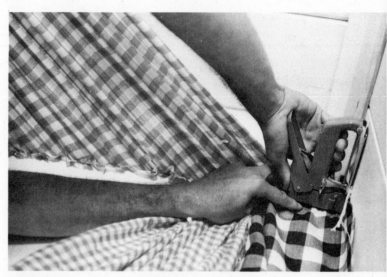

*Illus. 124*
Staple that end to the inside
of the adjoining wall.

*Illus. 125*
Pull the fabric out and begin
shirring lightly from
the opposite end.

*Illus. 126*
Knot these strings and staple to
the wall, allowing the fabric to
droop between the two staples.

*Illus. 127*
Start stapling the fabric all the way across the wall. As the stapling progresses, continue shirring to make certain that the folds are even. If there is any bunching or sagging at the end, simply tighten the knots in the shirring tape. Use lots of staples.

*Illus. 128*
The shirred wall at the ceiling line.

*Illus. 129*
Repeat steps in illus. 124–126 for bottom.

61

*Illus. 130*
Do not worry if the fabric does
not reach the floor; it will give
when it is pulled
tautly for stapling.

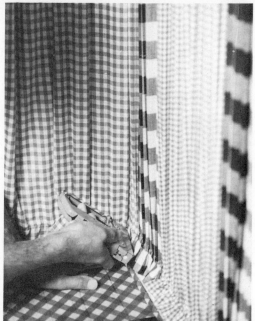

*Illus. 131*
Overlap the stapling slightly at
all corners to make sure that none
of the undersurface is visible.

*Illus. 132*
Locate the outlet and cut a slit
the same length.

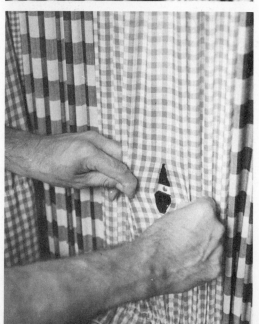

62

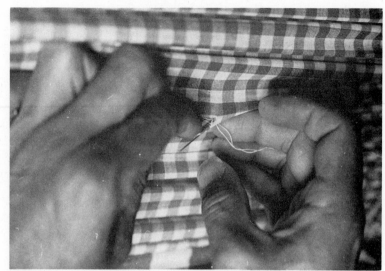

*Illus. 133*
Buttonhole stitch around the
slit to prevent raveling.

*Illus. 134*
The outlet in operation.

*Illus. 135*
The sliding-door end of the room.
It is done in three sections. The
fabric for either side of the window
is cut, pieced, and shirred
separately. The same procedure
is followed for the section
over the window.

*Illus. 136*
A short piece above or below a window or door is done exactly like the entire wall.

*Illus. 137*
The window. The sections above and below it are treated separately from the side sections. That comes to four separate units for this wall. It is very important to make certain that the gingham stripes are continuous— lined up above and below the window.

**The Door**

*Illus. 138*
The fabric necessary for a door is calculated and hung exactly as one does for a wall.

*Illus. 139*
Finishing the shirring at the top of a door. Notice how the stripes line up.

*Illus. 140*
The completed door.

*Illus. 141*
To cover a doorknob, cut a circle of fabric 3″ to 4″ wider than the diameter of the top of the knob. With about 12″ of heavy thread, stitch around the circle, staying about ½″ from the edge. Pull the thread so that the fabric forms a cap.

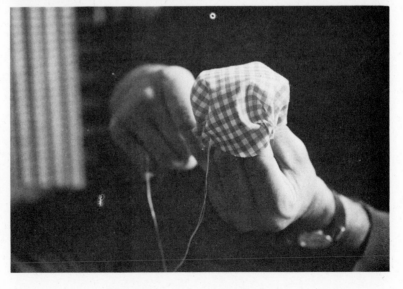

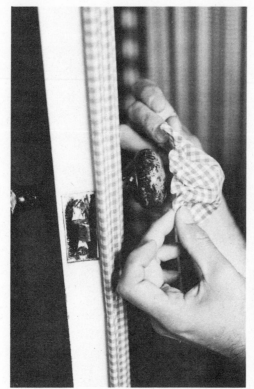

*Illus. 142*
Coat the doorknob with glue and
slip on the cap.

*Illus. 143*
Smooth out wrinkles and bubbles in the cap so
that it completely adheres to the knob.

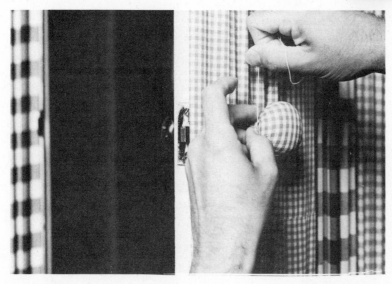

*Illus. 144*
Pull the threads tautly for a
really tight fit; then tie
them around the base.

## Curtains
### *Illus. 145*
The center of the wall shows the curtains which are loose at the bottom. They are done exactly as one would do a shirred wall— shirring only at the top. The gingham stripes follow the same pattern as those on the wall.

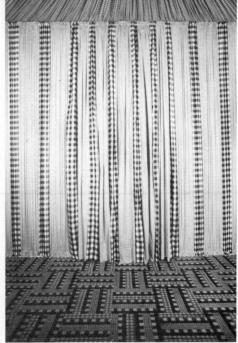

*Illus. 146*
Parting the curtains to tie them back. The stripe repeat order is kept in sequence on the section over the window.

*Illus. 147*
The window curtains tied back. Notice the section below; the order of the stripes is continued from the wall.

*Illus. 148*
The curtained sliding door. Notice the section above.

67

# Other Fabrics, Other Rooms

## Ahmet and Mica Ertegun Study

AHMET AND MICA ERTEGUN are among the most hospitable couples in New York City. They not only love to give parties, but they give some of the best around. The entire parlor floor of their handsome town house has been gutted and turned into one enormous reception room in which attractive conversation areas compete with a magnificent collection of contemporary paintings and sculpture.

When Mica designed the little upstairs room (*see* color insert, fig. 7), she realized that it would have to serve a dual function. It was to be a den that could also be used as an auxiliary guest room. The feeling of the room would have to be intimate, informal, and relaxed. Given her superlative taste, it would naturally also be extremely handsome.

The completed room is very lovely, but it is also the kind of place in which one would not hesitate to put one's feet up and be completely comfortable. A sense of balance dominates the room. English Regency furniture gives a note of hard elegance which offsets the fabric that dominates the room. Orange moldings warm the cool blue pattern that covers windows, couches, tables, and walls. The Oriental feeling of the fabric harmonizes with the European furniture. The richness of texture is muted by the neutral carpeting and ceiling. The accentuation of moldings lends a period definition to the timelessness of material.

Mica Ertegun selected a fabric that had a small pattern bordered by a larger pattern. The draperies had a large patterned border along the sides and top; when they were drawn, the smaller pattern was framed by the larger one. The ties are composed of fabric shirred on heavy cording. (To make them, *see* illus. 103–108.)

The twin sofas facing each other can be converted into beds. They were upholstered in the smaller pattern. The borders, which were cut off, were used to cover the little back pillows and to underscore the large seat pad.

Luis Perez covered the Parsons tables in front of the sofas in the tiny blue pattern. (To cover a Parson's table, *see* illus. 182–198.)

Although the walls look as if they were stretched, that was not the way they were applied. Actually, the way they were put up was much closer to the way a fabric floor is done than the customary handling of a wall.

The many moldings and doors broke up the walls into small areas, making it much easier for Luis to piece than to stretch. (Slatting and stretching a room with moldings necessitates removing the molding, outlining the area where they belong with slats, stretching the wall, and then replacing the moldings.) In addition to that, the entire wall on the left side of the desk (*see* illus. 149) was lined with closets which Mica Ertegun wanted to blend into the overall look of the room. To create this illusion with a stretched wall, the moldings would have

*Illus. 149*  Ertegun study

to be removed and treated with slats; all of the doors would have had to be outlined in slats and rehung, bringing the hinges out to the new wall level created by the slats.

Luis decided to dispense with the padding and glue the fabric directly to the wall. As most of the surface was to be covered with the part of the fabric containing the smaller pattern, the first thing he did was to cut off the large pattern border; this was reserved for later use in the panels. Using a rolling pan and roller (a small brush for corners and angles), he put up the trimmed fabric exactly as one would hang wallpaper. The only difference was that he used the white household glue instead of wallpaper paste. He took as much care with stray threads here as he did with a floor.

After the basic wall was completed, he glued the border over it to serve as a border within the larger panels. He also used some border to completely fill those narrower panels which had none of the smaller pattern covering.

## Rafael Cobian Den

Another Perez blue den is in the Park Avenue apartment of Mr. and Mrs. Rafael Cobian (*see* color insert, fig. 8). When the Cobians are alone, the room provides a comfortable retreat for reading and watching television. At large parties, the drapes are drawn, small tables are set up, flowers are placed everywhere, and soft lights illumine the room, flickering in the chiaroscuro folds of the shirred walls and tented ceiling. Mrs. Cobian has said, "On those nights, the room reminds the guests of the intimate *boîtes de nuit* one used to visit in Paris."

The room has many interesting features from the point of view of fabric. The shirred walls are made of two different printed fabrics which were sewn together. The walls are hung on rods so that they can be taken down, and they are only shirred on top. This enabled Luis Perez to conceal a row of closets and a door which led to another part of the apartment (*see* illus. 150).

In illustration 151, the area behind the shirred wall is visible. Access to the door on the left was made possible by tying the shirred wall back with shirred cording (*see* illus. 152); the

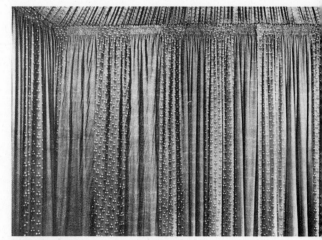

Illus. 150

Illus. 151

Illus. 152

Fig. 1. The gingham room

Fig. 2. Ahmet and Mica Erteghun bedroom floor

Fig. 3. Patchwork floor

Fig. 4. Gingham room floor

Fig. 5. Quilt floor in the Kent Kleinman nursery

Fig. 6.  Tented ceiling

Fig. 7.  Ahmet and
          Mica Erteghun study

Fig. 8. Rafael Cobian shirred wall and tented ceiling

Fig. 9.  Tracy Swope bedroom

Fig. 10. Zajac and Callahan bedroom

Fig. 11. Mr. and Mrs. Dwight Hemmion sitting room

Fig. 12. Mr. and Mrs. William Rayner sitting room

Fig. 13. Chessy Rayner bathroom walls

Fig. 14. Zajac and Callahan bathroom

Fig. 15. Bill Blass dining room

Fig. 16.  Kenneth Lane dining room

Fig. 18. Famolare showroom

Fig. 19. Geraldine Stutz elevator

Fig. 20. Parsons table

Fig. 21. Desk and desk chair

Fig. 22. Divan

Fig. 24. Television

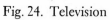

Fig. 23. Armchair

Fig. 25. Telephone

latter was also used on the window drapes. The wall over the closets (on the right) was hung on a traverse rod so that it could be opened and closed with a drawstring.

The tent was hung exactly like the one in the gingham fabric room (*see* illus. 112–121). The elaborate rosette (*see* illus. 153) was built up of ribbon and cording made of the two printed fabrics used in the walls.

As a finishing touch, Luis Perez created some accessories for Mrs. Cobian. Illustration 154 shows the address book that he covered with

*Illus. 153*

*Illus. 154*

*Illus. 155*

some of the wall fabric. A pencil cup, letter opener and pen, all covered in wall fabric, can be seen in illustration 155.

## Tracy Swope Bedroom

Tracy Swope, the extremely gifted and popular young actress, is the daughter of Herbert Bayard and Maggie Hayes Swope. She lives with her parents in a rambling apartment in New York City's Upper East Side. When she landed a leading role in a television serial, she asked Luis Perez to redo her conventional bedroom so that it could also function as a sitting room and den.

Tracy wanted a pretty, feminine look, one which could be created on a limited budget. To save on the cost of fabric, Luis used sheets with a floral pattern for the stretched walls, tented ceiling, and bedspread. He made the headboard and footboard for the bed by first covering pieces of plywood with the fabric and then bolting them to the box spring. Even the bookshelves and radiator case were covered with the sheets. To do the walls, it was simply a question of staple and stretch. The result is a room that looks extravagant and is as feminine as Tracy could possibly have wished, yet one that was created in a most economical fashion (*see* color insert, fig. 9).

To hang the chandelier, Luis made the rosette and hung the tent. Instead of covering the entire rosette with fabric, however, he left the center over the pipe and flanges open and suspended the lighting fixture through it.

charming bedroom created by Zajac and Callahan (*see* color insert, fig. 10) are an example of this attention to the little finishing fillip. After they were stapled and stretched, Luis used some blue shirred ribbon along the top and bottom. Not only did it cover his staples; it also added a distinctive accent that made the walls more attractive.

*Illus. 156*

The detail of the room (*see* illus. 156) reveals several interesting facets of Luis' work in this room. The windows had rather interesting moldings; Luis simply glued the fabric over them, sculpting the material with his fingers to make certain that the architectural features were not lost. He covered his staples by gluing a double row of cording (made from the sheeting) over them. The bookcase was taken apart, covered (for covering shelves, *see* illus. 57–64), and then reassembled.

The richness of craft exhibited in rooms like Tracy Swope's bedroom is the trademark of Luis Perez. In doing a room, the absolutely finished look more than compensates for the extra time and effort expended on the little things.

The work of Perez abounds in the small touches that make all the difference in the completed room. The walls he executed in the

For sheer loveliness, few rooms can compete with the sitting room decorated by Zajac and Callahan in a Victorian summer cottage in Ouoque, Long Island (*see* color insert, fig. 11). When Mr. and Mrs. Dwight Hemmion commissioned the room, they wanted a room that would be soft, comfortable, informal and able to accommodate as many guests as they might choose to invite. The decorators more than fulfilled their requirements in the completed, two-patterned room.

There are several novel details to be noted in the shirred walls and curtains executed by Luis Perez. The walls are shirred only at the top and hang freely to the top of the whitewashed baseboards, thus retaining the architectural integrity of the room. To finish off the bottoms, Luis pasted cording, made of the wall fabric, above the baseboards.

The treatment of the windows is another example of using fabric and still being true to the essential feeling of the room. Between them, the fabric is hung in panels, leaving the original frames open to view. The curtains are on rods so·that they can be drawn in the evening. The three ties are both visually pleasing and practical, as they allow as much light as possible into the room during the day.

## Rayner Sitting Room and Bathroom

The Southampton sitting room of Mr. and Mrs. William Rayner is another example of a handsome treatment of a summer home. Given this setting, the great taste of Chessy Rayner worked with an enviable sense of the economics of a limited budget (see color insert, fig. 12).

The walls and window shades are covered with inexpensive Indian cotton saris. In addition to costing very little, the brilliance of the patterns eliminated the need for drapes.

To execute the shades, Perez cut two of the saris to match the length and width of the shades, carefully preserving the dominant motif of the tree equidistant from the sides of each piece of fabric. The cut lengths of material were then glued to the shades with spray rubber cement. The position of the trees was again important. They were placed at a distance from the bottom of the shades that brought them to the same height as the trees on the walls (when the shades were pulled down).

The fabric was glued directly to the walls as it had been in Mica Ertegun's den. Because the saris were not large enough to cover the entire wall areas in which they had been placed, Luis created a new design that was super-imposed on the original fabrics.

He cut borders from other fabrics. After the trees were centered on the walls, these borders were used to build out to the sides, ceiling, and floor. Border after border was glued down until the entire wall was covered.

The treatment around the door, partially visible at the left of the photo, is particularly decorative. The border surrounding the tree in the original fabric was cut off and pasted to frame the entrance; the other borders were used to build out exactly as they were in the other wall panels.

Note the logic with which the outer borders are continued over the window; the original small fabrics give the illusion of being much larger, with many concentric designs running around the central tree patterns.

Old bathrooms with bad walls and ancient plumbing fixtures are generally considered design disaster areas. People either tear everything out and start from scratch or make do as best they can with generally insufficient decorative compromises. For anyone versed in the craft of "fabric-cation," this need not be the case.

Chessy Rayner's New York apartment is in a lovely old building. The plumbing fixtures in her bathroom are as old as the rest of the place, but not quite as lovely. The tub and sink are commodious in a fashion that is almost non-existent in contemporary counterparts; Mrs. Rayner did not want to part with them when she was redecorating the flat. Instead, she decided to make the rest of the small room as striking as possible to compensate for their appearance.

Luis Perez was called upon to do the walls. He framed out the room in slats and stretched a handsome striped fabric across the walls. To add an unusual note, the fabric was stretched on the bias (see color insert, fig. 13).

While in the process of doing the walls, the medicine chest was removed and a mirror later hung in its place. The problem of storage was solved by using straw baskets set upon shelves suspended on chromium runners. A modern three-part lighting fixture completed a bathroom that utilized modern design concepts to compensate for out-of-date essentials. It was all done so simply that most home crafters faced with the same problems can easily duplicate the solution without any outside help.

## Zajac and Callahan Bathroom

When Zajac and Callahan did an old-fashioned bathroom, they decided to play up its dated look to give the room a feeling that was almost Victorian (see color insert, fig. 14).

The Victorian age was an eclectic one. The

decorators realized this splendidly in the choice of accessories. Art Nouveau butterflies were suspended from the ceiling, colorful Mexican paper fans festooned the walls, a rococo mirror with shell-motif frame was hung over a bamboo hamper. The overall feeling was that of an eccentric collector who was unafraid to mix and mingle objects gathered from everywhere and every period.

The fabric selected was a bold red imprinted with fin de siècle fans and tiny flowers which evoked the spirit of an age gone by. To give the illusion of lowering the extremely high ceiling, it was decided that the fabric would stop at a molding about six feet from the floor. Luis Perez shirred it on rods so that the material could be removed for laundering in case of soap stains and splashing from sink and tub.

The fabric skirt around the tub also had to be removable for cleaning. It would be extremely difficult to hang it on rods since these would have to be bolted to the porcelain-coated iron fixture. Luis solved the problem by pasting one strip of Velcro just under the lip of the tub. He gathered the skirt on shirring tape and sewed the other Velcro strip to the shirring tape.

The treatment of the bathtub was another example of the utilization of the marvelous contemporary materials available to us. When any special difficulties arise, such as this skirt or the hollow pipe necessary for a ceiling rosette, Luis has generally found that a visit to a hardware store or notions department will turn up a practical solution. "Fabric-cators" or any other kind of crafters should make it a practice to stop in at these specialty shops. A browse will often turn up some wonderful gadget that will be very useful in the practice of their crafts.

## Bill Blass Dining Room

Bachelors are great diners-in. After marriage, a wife is forever fixing up a den or toolroom for the man of the house. In the life of a single man, next to his bedroom, an attractive dining area is the most strategic part of his apartment or house.

There are many reasons why this is true. Bachelors are often excellent cooks, an art they seldom practice after their wedding but delight in displaying before that fateful day. On occasion, they have to give dinner parties to pay back the many invitations that they have accepted, for there is nothing more sought-after than a charming extra man. And, of course, an intimate dinner for two with wine, candlelight, and soft music is one of the greatest ploys in the strategy of seduction.

Two of the most attractive bachelors around are the well-known costume jewelry designer, Kenneth Lane, and his equally famous colleague in clothing design, Bill Blass. The New York bases of both these gentlemen were designed by Mac II.

Mr. Blass makes his home in a handsome penthouse in New York City's fashionable Sutton Place area. His dining room is an elegant little jewel box wrapped in a brilliant English yellow print chintz (see color insert, fig. 15). The decorators saved a great deal of valuable space by setting the dining table in a corner before an upholstered banquette rather than placing it squarely in the center of the small room.

Luis Perez lined the walls in flannel. The room was framed out in slats and the fabric stretched in the manner already described. The stapled corners were masked by heavy cording made of the wall fabric.

The treatment of the closet doors in the Blass dining room is an example of Perez's sleight of hand. By the time he had finished, they had almost disappeared into the walls (see illus. 157). Luis pasted the fabric directly onto

Illus. 157

the doors, covering the surrounding moldings and frames. When using a printed material, the important thing in duplicating this trick is to make certain that all the repeats line up perfectly with the repeats in the walls around the doors.

Although it looks like a normal recess, the wall opposite the dining table presented a special problem. (*See* illus. 158; note the Parsons table covered with the wall fabric.)

The rear is actually a panel that can be removed (*see* illus. 159). The real wall contains a fuse box. It would have been impossible to stretch fabric directly over it without creating what would have resembled a patch to cover the box lid. Instead, Luis built a slatted wooden frame the size of the wall. The fabric was stretched over it. (*See* illus. 160, which shows the rear of the frame with its many support bars.) In this instance, both fabric and padding were stretched right over the edges and stapled to the narrow sides of the slats. When it was completed, the panel easily slid into place and lifted away to give access to the fuse box. In position, it became an invisible part of the wall; the repeats in the panel precisely

*Illus. 158*

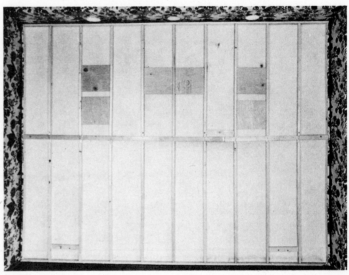

*Illus. 160*

matched the repeats in the surrounding wall areas.

*Illus. 159*

## Kenneth Lane Dining Room

Kenneth Lane's town house is a study in contradictions. It functions both as a residence and a base for his extremely successful costume jewelry business. The dining room, with its magnificent Perez tent and walls (*see* color insert, fig. 16), also serves as a card room and music room. It has a wonderful sense of fantasy about it. Shirred walls part to reveal bookcases, mirrors, and a fireplace. Mr. Lane has said, "I've wanted a tented room ever since a visit I made to Egypt several years ago. There, near the pyramids, they set up the most fabulous tents. You can rent them for dinner parties. Musicians come in and play. I wanted to capture some of that exoticism right here in this room. Call it recollections of the wilder shores of love."

Dim lighting, stacks of cushions, banquettes, mock pillows, taboret tables—they all contribute to the desired evocation of a fantasy oasis. Mr. Lane also admitted, "I do adore tents. If I had a funky kind of railroad flat apartment, I'd just have the room done as a series of tents, one leading into another. It'd be heaven."

Despite the aura of a luxurious never-never land, the tented ceiling and walls served a very practical function. Lane later explained, "Aside from the question of personal taste, it has a purpose. The floors are tiled, and every sound is magnified by them. Not something to be desired in a room that functions as a sometime card room, a sometime music room, and a sometime dining room. Conventional soundproofing materials are so ugly. Fabric does the job as well, and it's beautiful."

Hanging the Lane tent posed some problems for Luis Perez. The largest was that there were chandeliers at both ends of the room. As a result, he did not have one focal point from which he could stretch the fabric to the walls. The solution arrived at was to hang a strip of 1" by 2" lumber between the two rosettes and lighting fixtures. He hung the fabric from the 1" by 2" the entire length of each of the long walls running parallel to it.

To do this, he gathered the two lots of material necessary for each wall. They were sewn to each other and then to a shirring tape. The shirring tape seam was shortened to the length of the 1" by 2" and stapled to it. The shirring tape cords were tied around the flange-ended pipes of the rosettes. The linked lengths of fabric were stretched to the appropriate walls. The pie-shaped wedges radiating from the rosettes to the shorter walls were hung in the conventional manner.

Another problem was posed by the heating and air-conditioning ducts that lined the walls just beneath the ceiling. They had to be covered yet still permit the free passage of air currents. A fringed skirt was made for the tent and stapled to it all around the room. It masked the ducts but still allowed them to function. The

*Illus. 161*

shirred walls were hung on rods that were also hidden by the skirt (*see* illus. 161).

## Francine Coffey Office

The use of fabric in decoration is not restricted to the home. It can also greatly enhance the ambiance of office, shop, or showroom. Luis Perez's work in Francine Coffey's office is an example of how fabric can be used to transform the sterile atmosphere of modern offices into something warm and visually striking.

Miss Coffey is a vital and imaginative young executive with the Singer Sewing Machine Company. She called upon Luis to help with the decoration of the bare, straight-lined, rectangular room that was to be her base in the New York headquarters of the firm. When the job was finished, she had an office that was true to contemporary structural elements yet still managed to be extremely personal in feeling and concept (*see* color insert, fig. 17).

An inexpensive brown cotton suede was used to cover the walls and ceiling. Since there was no pattern or grain to worry about, it was both easy and economical to work with.

The wall fabric was simply sewn together and pasted directly onto the walls without slatting or stapling. When applying a wall in this fashion, one must be certain that the surface is smooth; cracks and defects will show through. The crafting trick to remember is that one should not so much stretch as pat down the fabric in the same way that one does with a fabric floor.

The ceiling was framed out in slats and stretched. The stapled seams were covered with hollow aluminum tubing bolted into the slats. In addition to hiding the seams, the tubing also served to conceal the electrical wiring. Aluminum trim was used for the doors of the folding closet upon which the fabric had been pasted.

## Famolare Showroom

The Famolare Shoe Company manufactures some of the most daring and fashionable footwear in the country. For their showroom they wanted a look as posh and elegant as their footwear. Interior designer Billy Giblin suggested a luscious, bold red print. He called upon Luis Perez to execute the walls and cover the Parsons tables.

Shirring tape was sewn to the fabric and stapled to the walls. An added opulence was achieved by the bountiful use of fabric. It was draped over windows, arches, and even the mirror. Shirred cording ties were used to pull it back. The richness of the result served as a marvelous balance to the display of the vivid shoes with their hard-edged designs (see color insert, fig. 18).

## Geraldine Stutz Elevator

When Geraldine Stutz and her husband William Gibbs leased a new duplex apartment in the top floors of a Manhattan town house, everything about their new abode pleased them except the access to the apartment. The small, unadorned elevator car was the sort that the French facetiously call "vertical coffins."

Beyond that, it took a seemingly interminable length of time to rise from the street-floor level to their quarters, a period passed with only an open, grill gate to separate the passengers from a bleak vista of cinder blocks. It was a trip that in no way prepared the visitor for the splendidly cheerful living room, hung with examples of the gifted Mr. Gibbs's own paintings.

Miss Stutz did not want hard-edged elegance in the carriage, nor did she want a landscape of gray or even-colored cinder blocks. She fancied a patterned, comfortable softness that would prepare the passenger for the warmth that awaited him/her in the home above. In short, she wanted fabric.

From her first associations with Luis Perez, back in their I. Miller days, she knew that if you wanted fabric, you called Perez. They started planning the décor of both the elevator and the shaft.

Miss Stutz wanted the walls of the car to have such a quality of softness that they would look as if one could sink into them. Luis nodded approvingly, knowing exactly what he would do and how he would go about doing it (see illus. 162–175). By the time he had completed the car, Gerry Stutz was jocularly calling it "my private padded cell" (see color insert, fig. 19).

"Fabric-cating" the shaft was something else again. Before Luis Perez and Geraldine Stutz put their heads together, one can safely say that nobody had ever thought of papering an elevator shaft, let alone covering it with fabric.

The problem was how to cover the part of the shaft that was exposed through the elevator gates. Luis took a stop-and-go ride on the top of the elevator car. Along the way he carefully measured all of the spaces between the floors and around the doors.

Wooden frames were constructed to these dimensions. Onto these frames Luis stretched the same fabric used to cover the interior of the car. It was the same process used to make the panel wall in Bill Blass's dining room. When they were completely covered, the frames were bolted in place in the shaft wall (see illus. 176–178).

## The Fabric Elevator

*Illus. 162*
The elevator car before the application of fabric. Plywood has been bolted to the metal walls to facilitate stapling.

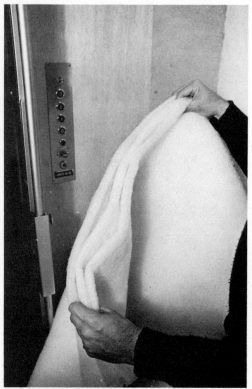

*Illus. 163*
Three layers of dacron batting are used to line the walls.

*Illus. 164*
Staple the dacron (all three layers) together along the ceiling and down the sides.

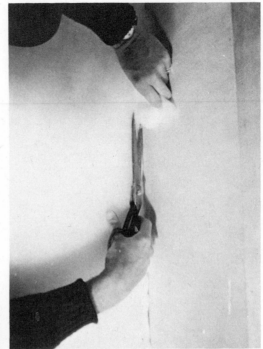

*Illus. 165*
Trim excess dacron from sides.

*Illus. 166*
Staple dacron along the
floor and trim.

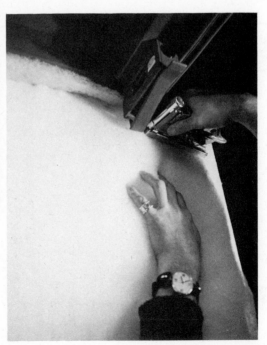

*Illus. 167*
Repeat steps in illus. 163–166 for all
four walls: be especially careful not to
interfere with the functioning
of mechanical devices.

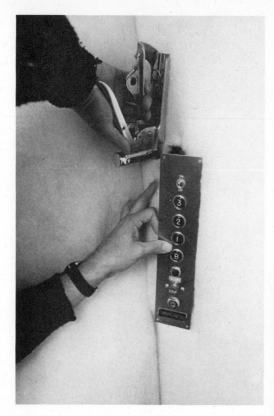

*Illus. 168*
Before attempting to do the control panel wall, loosen panel, cut dacron around opening; staple dacron right to the edge of the opening so that it remains under the panel when it is rebolted.

*Illus. 169*
Doing one wall at a time, cut, staple, stretch, and trim the fabric over the batting liner.

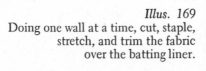

*Illus. 170*
Cut and staple around the control panel.

*Illus.* 171
Trim the control panel with cording.

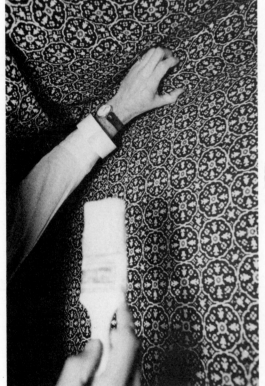

*Illus.* 172
Glue the fabric directly to the metal ceiling and trim with a razor blade at the wall angle.

*Illus.* 173
Find the outline of the lighting fixture under the ceiling fabric. Using a razor blade, make diagonal cuts from corner to corner and then trim around the sides.

*Illus. 174*
Detail of corner of the car showing cording used to hide the seams.

*Illus. 175*
Detail of covering of mechanical device of the gate track.

## The Elevator Shaft

*Illus. 176*
View of the shaft from the top of the elevator
car, showing the fabric panels in place.

*Illus. 177*
Riding up in the fabric shaft.

*Illus. 178*
Detail of the shaft through
the gate.

A fabric elevator shaft is not a project recommended for most home-crafters. Riding up and down on the top of an elevator car is not everybody's idea of fun, but it is the sort of project that challenges and delights Luis Perez.

Doing a closet is not unlike doing an elevator car. The same principles of applying fabric are employed, except for the fact that it is not padded; that would take up too much precious hanging space. Even problem closets, like the one in the gingham room, are easy to do once one learns the principles of applying material to a wall (see illus. 47-80).

These basics of fabric crafting are easy enough to learn, but it is the detail that really tells the story. The small things are what make the difference between doing a wall in the Perez manner and simply applying material to one. In these matters, Luis' overall concern is fidelity to the repeats in patterns. It may take more fabric to make certain that the repeats are aligned, but there is a world of difference in the result. It is the subtle finishing touch that is the mark of good craftsmanship. It is not difficult to do. It simply takes a little more time, a little more effort, and a little more fabric.

When completing a room, heating registers are certainly details that must be treated with care, as was the case with the gingham floor (see illus. 28-30). To apply fabric to a register that is located on the wall, use the same method.

Even after the job seems finished, take another close look at the room. Something may occur to you that will add a lovely last note. It might be covering the chain holding a chandelier with shirred fabric (see illus. 179) or adding a strip of fabric within a molding (see illus. 180). Doing everything in fabric is often no more than opening oneself to the possibilities that already exist.

Illus. 179

Illus. 180

# "Fabric-cated" Furniture

TRUE TO HIS original plan, Luis Perez covered every stick of furniture in the fabric room with gingham. The condition of the pieces before he covered them was of little importance. The only thing that mattered was that they be sturdy; no wobbling tables or desk chairs upon which one could not sit without fear of having them collapse. Aside from that, they could be covered with scratches, have dreadful finishes, or upholstery that was coming apart at the seams. It did not concern Luis, for none of it would be visible.

Any nondescript piece from the unfinished furniture store can become a thing of beauty when treated with fabric. Actually, the less value the things have, the better suited they are for this purpose. One would not want to cover furniture that had real worth or was made of marvelous wood.

What a wonderful thing "fabric-cation" is for "junk" furniture—old, discarded, or overlooked objects. A careful search of attic, storeroom, or basement will usually turn up all manner of odds and ends of furniture that can have new life when done in material.

Before investing money in a new table or chair, one should invest the small amount of time necessary to take a fresh look at discards. A little ingenuity and a few yards of fabric can result in a striking piece of furniture that cannot be duplicated at any price in a store. Not only will it make a handsome and unusual ad-

dition to a room, but doing it will give the crafter that special sense of accomplishment which never comes from merely spending money—a trick that almost anybody who has it can perform well.

With the exception of the television and a desk lamp (that came from Woolworth's), all of the furnishings in the gingham room were purchased at a used furniture store. The total expenditure was under $100.

The little Parsons table is an excellent place to start one's adventures in fabric and furniture. Its lines are clean and straight. There are no moldings, ridges, or embellishments. The whole job can be done in a couple of hours.

This table has a lovely shape of almost classical simplicity. With just the slightest smattering of carpentry know-how, it can be made at home. It can certainly be purchased for very little money at almost any unpainted furniture store.

Covering a Parsons table with fabric creates a change in feeling by counterpointing the simplicity of line with a richness of texture and color. For the gingham room, Luis covered the Parson's table in blue gingham (*see* color insert, fig. 20); he has also covered them in chintz, heavy drapery fabric, and even in an East Indian carpet (*see* illus. 181).

Once you've mastered the simple basics of doing one of these tables, it's possible to experiment with all manner of variations. (For

*Illus. 181*

instructions on how to cover a Parsons table, *see* illus. 182–198.) For example, one can do a pieced Parsons table by following the same design principles used in doing a pieced floor. Appliqués can be incorporated to marvelous effect. Legs can be covered in contrasting colors and patterns.

It is possible to use urethane or shellac and varnish on fabric-covered furniture just as one might on a floor. It will certainly protect the surfaces against damage and dirt. If the matte finish of fabric is preferred, these protective coats are not necessary on the legs of tables and chairs. However, any flat surface (a table or

**The Parsons Table**
*Illus. 182*
The Parsons table covered with a coat of white paint. Even if the table is raw wood, it's a good idea to give it a coat of paint. This goes for all furniture that is "fabric-cated."

*Illus. 183*
Cut a piece of fabric the combined length of the table and its legs. Coat the top of the table with glue; centering the fabric on the tabletop, paste it down, taking care to gingerly smooth out all wrinkles, bubbles, and distortions in the pattern.

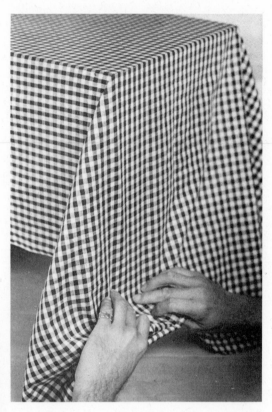

*Illus. 184*
Coat one short side plus legs with glue and paste the fabric down.

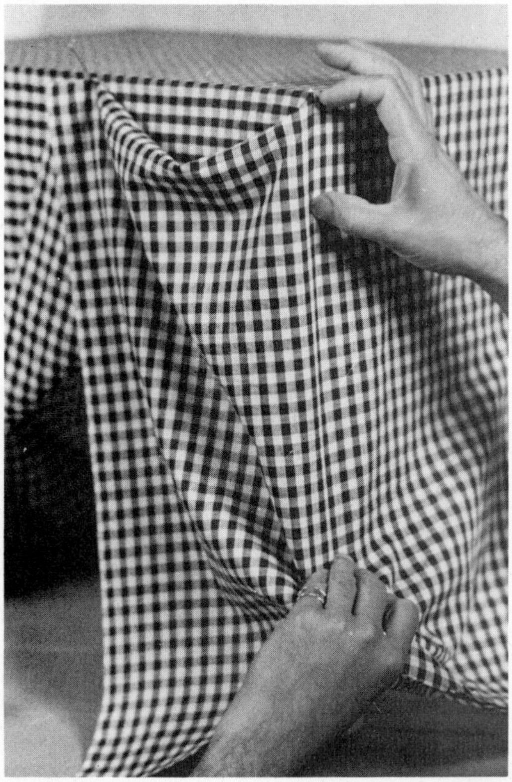

*Illus. 185*
Pin the excess fabric to the longer sides (this will get it out of your way) and continue smoothing the fabric. Add more glue if necessary.

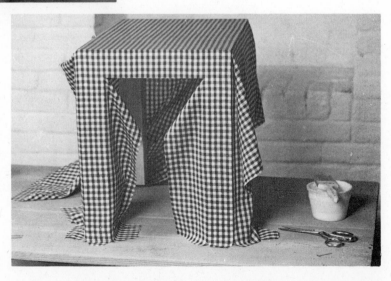

*Illus. 186*
Cut up the center of the fabric to the top and then along the edges to the legs. *Don't cut down the legs.* Repeat steps in illus. 184–186 for the other short side.

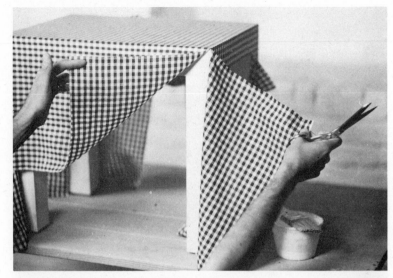

*Illus. 187*
Unpin the fabric on one of
the longer sides. Hold it out in a
straight line (at each leg);
cut along the top surface
to the corner.

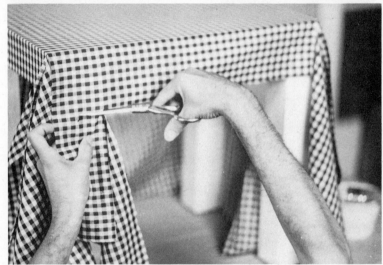

*Illus. 188*
Trim the excess fabric just below
the lower edge of the tabletop.

*Illus. 189*
Fold the flap (made in illus. 188)
over the top of the table. Using
a straightedge and a razor
blade, carefully cut a diagonal line
from top to bottom corners on
both sides. Apply glue to the
legs and paste the fabric down.

*Illus.* 190
Using a brush, apply glue to the area between the "fabric-cated" legs. Lift the flap and paste it down, being careful to keep it smooth.

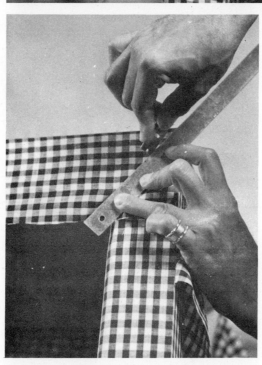

*Illus.* 191
The diagonal cut made in illus. 189 will be visible through the fabric flap. Place a straightedge alongside the first diagonal and make another slit.

*Illus.* 192
Remove the excess fabric.

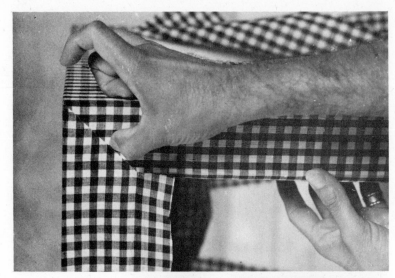

*Illus. 193*
If the joins in the diagonal cuts do not quite meet, the fabric will give enough for them to be pushed together. Apply glue under the side of the table; paste the extra little bit of fabric made in illus. 188 down under it. Repeat steps in illus. 187–193 for the other side of the table.

*Illus. 194*
Turn the table upside down and start to trim and glue the fabric around the legs.

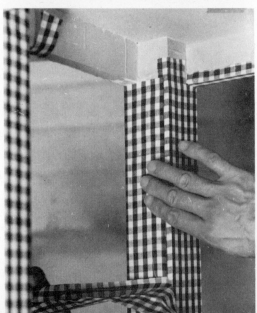

*Illus. 195*
There will be a great deal of fabric to trim. The wraparounds should meet at the back of the legs, but they should not overlap.

*Illus. 196*
Trim the fabric at the bottoms
of the legs, leaving an inch;
make slits at the corners.

*Illus. 197*
Apply glue and paste flaps down.

*Illus. 198*
Apply glue to all loose threads.
Allow them to dry; then snip
off the stiffened threads.

desk top) on which drinks, food, or other stainables are going to be placed must have some protection; a stain on natural fabric is going to be there forever. A piece of glass, lucite, or clear plastic cut to the dimensions of the surface will do excellently.

Luis' red gingham desk chair is one of the best-looking things in the fabric room. Actually, it's one of those old ladder-back kitchen chairs that used to be so popular not too long ago. A search through junk shops and attics will probably turn up dozens. A fantastic change is wrought by fabric (*see* color insert, fig. 21). (For instructions, *see* illus. 199–224.)

### The Kitchen/Desk Chair
*Illus. 199*
The kitchen chair. If it is not already white, give it a coat of flat white paint.

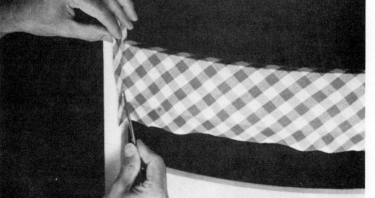

*Illus. 200*
Cut a piece of fabric, on the bias, large enough to wrap around the top rung of the chair. Coat the rung with glue and apply the fabric to it, leaving the seam at the bottom. Use a pin to push the fabric into the corners.

*Illus. 201*
Using a razor blade, trim away excess fabric at bottom and sides.

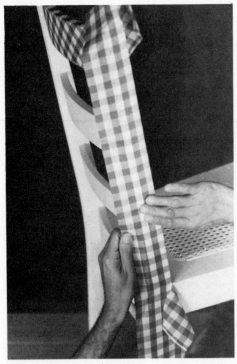

*Illus.* 202
Cut a piece of fabric long enough
to cover the entire length of the rear
vertical support and wide enough
to wrap around it. Glue it to the
side surface. (Notice that this fabric is
not cut on the bias. One of the
things that adds interest to the
"fabric-cation" of a chair is to cut all
horizontals on the bias and
all verticals naturally.)

*Illus.* 203
Trim fabric around seat and
bar beneath it.

*Illus.* 204
Glue fabric to rear of vertical support.

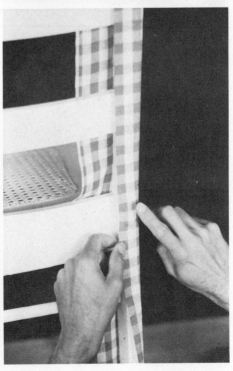

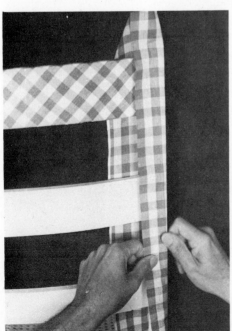

*Illus.* 205
Glue it around at the top until it
meets the horizontal bars.

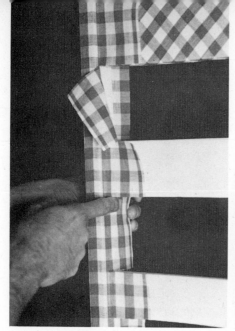

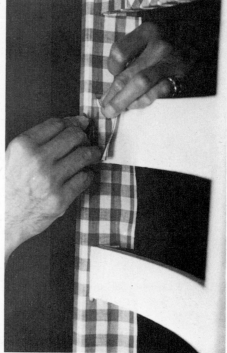

*Illus. 206*
For the front of the backrest, make slits at the horizontal bars.

*Illus. 207*
Glue the cut fabric around the horizontals and trim. The seam should be precisely at that point at the rear of the bars where the fabric ends meet.

*Illus. 208*
Trim the fabric at the top, making sure to leave about 1", and cut slits at corners. Fold the newly formed flaps down over each other (as if one were closing a carton) and glue.

*Illus. 209*
Cut and trim fabric near seat so that it will come up and around in the rear to meet the backrest fabric.

*Illus.* 210
Glue around seat and cut in a circular
fashion around the rear dowel.

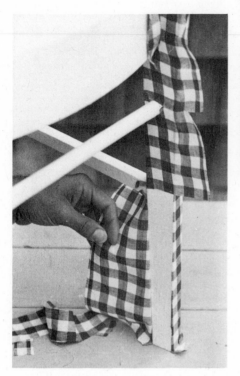

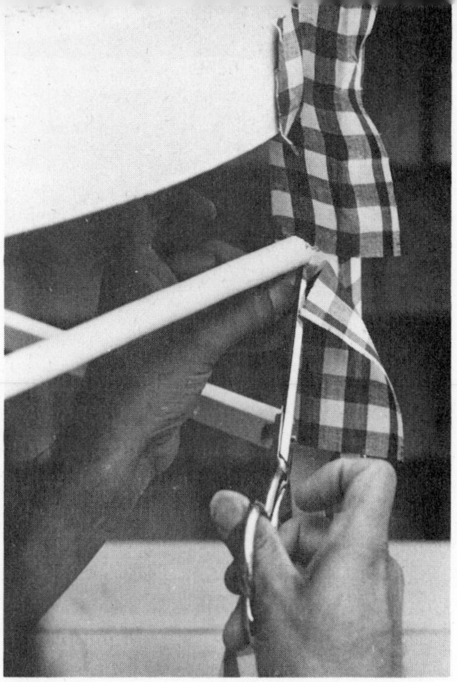

*Illus.* 211
Glue around the dowel and repeat
around the side bar.

*Illus.* 212
Trim all excess fabric. Treat bottom of
leg exactly as top of vertical support was
treated. (*See* illus. 208.) Repeat steps
in illus. 202–212 with other
vertical support.

*Illus.* 213
At front leg, paste a piece of fabric
from under the seat to bottom of leg,
cutting the flaps that will eventually
seal the bottom.

95

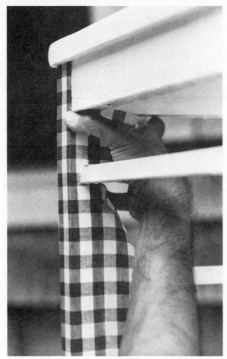

*Illus. 214*
Cut, glue, and trim around seat and
supports exactly as was done with
rear vertical support. Seal flaps at bottom.

*Illus. 215*
Cut fabric on the bias and wrap, glue,
and trim around all lower horizontal
bars and dowels. This is no different from
doing top horizontal bars. The seam
should be at the bottom.

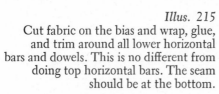

*Illus. 216*
Repeat steps in illus. 199–201 for all
backrest horizontal rungs.

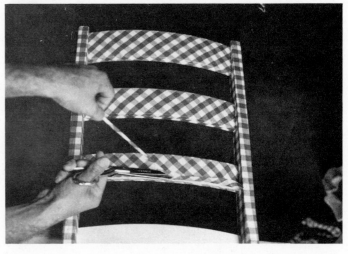

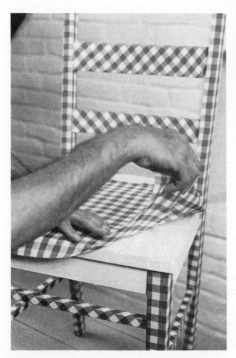

*Illus. 217*
Paste a piece of fabric over the seat.

*Illus. 218*
Trim at the rear of the seat.

*Illus. 219*
Outline the perimeter of the cane seating
in pencil. Cut along the pencil
line and remove the fabric.

*Illus. 220*
Make slits at corners of fabric covering seat.

*Illus. 221*
Glue fabric around rim of seat and trim.

*Illus. 222*
Cut, glue, wrap, and trim
bias-cut fabric around the front,
sides, and rear faces of the seat.
For the rear, begin covering
process at edge of seat and bring
it around and under.

*Illus. 223*
Bottom view of chair, showing
how fabric is brought around
and glued under.

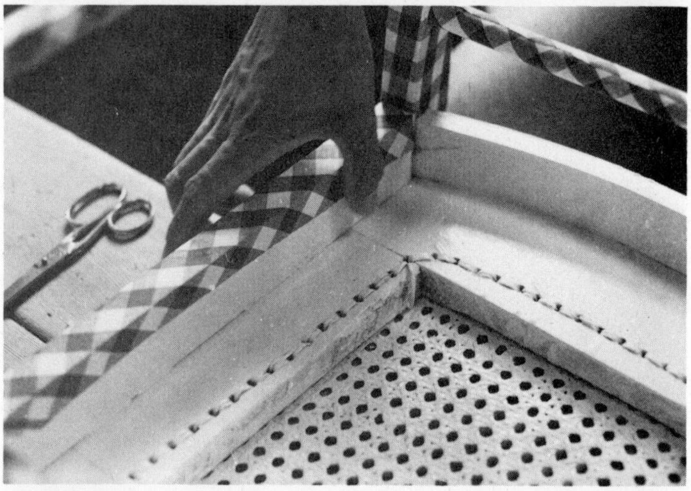

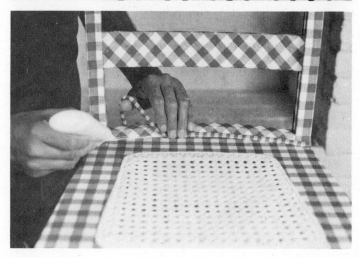

*Illus. 224*
Trim rear of seat with cording
made of same fabric.

The gingham room desk was very easy to cover (*see* color insert, fig. 21). It was not much more difficult than the Parsons table. This is true of any straight-lined piece. If the desk has any molding or gilt, it can be handled the same way the gingham room mirror was treated. (For detailed instructions, *see* illus. 225–248.)

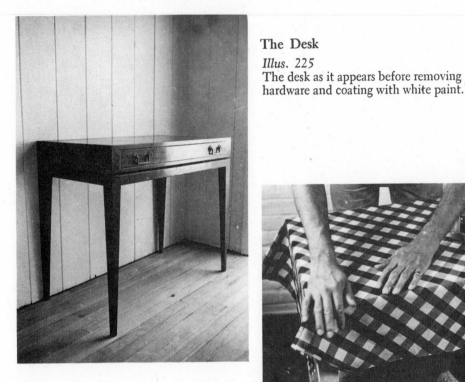

## The Desk

*Illus. 225*
The desk as it appears before removing hardware and coating with white paint.

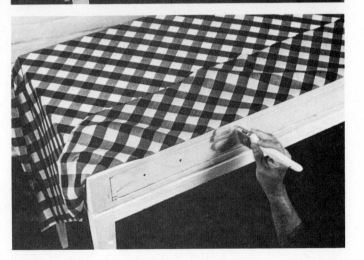

*Illus. 226*
Cut a piece of fabric large enough to cover top surface and sides of boxlike upper portion of the desk. Apply glue to top; paste and smooth down fabric.

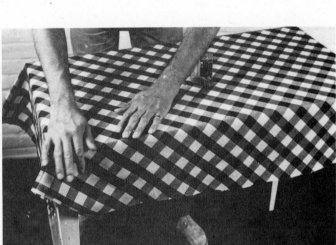

*Illus. 227*
Apply glue and paste down right over the drawer.

Illus. 228
Use a razor blade to cut around
the drawer.

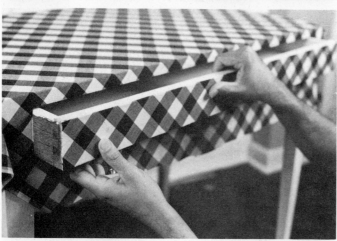

Illus. 229
Remove the drawer and lay it aside.

Illus. 230
Apply glue to indentation. Use a straightedge
to push the fabric into indentation, making
sure that it adheres. Trim away excess
fabric. Repeat for all sides.

Illus. 231
Cut away excess fabric at corners. Apply
some glue with brush at corners and
around drawer opening to stiffen loose
threads. Cut them away.

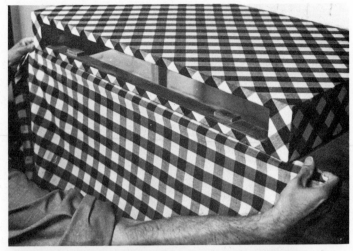

*Illus. 232*
Cut a piece of fabric large enough to cover the entire lower half of the front of the desk to a little longer than the floor and wrap one-third of the way around the sides.

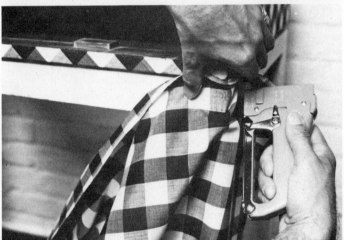

*Illus. 233*
Use a few staples to attach the fabric to the sides. They'll be removed later.

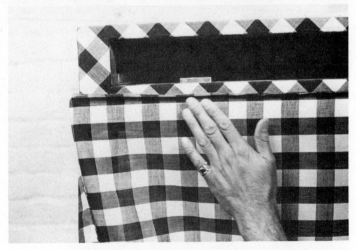

*Illus. 234*
Apply glue to indentation, as well as the area just beneath it, and smooth fabric in and down.

*Illus. 235*
Cut away most of the fabric between the legs, leaving more than double the legs' width at each leg.

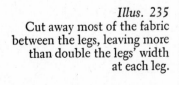

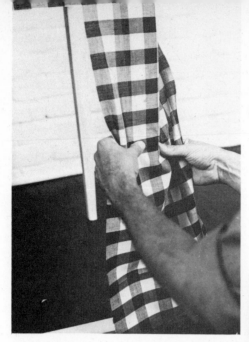

*Illus. 236*
Glue the fabric to the legs.

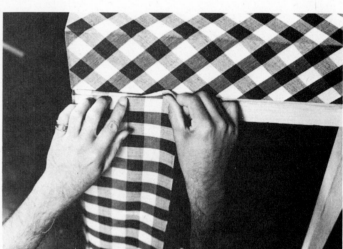

*Illus. 237*
Remove the side staples; apply glue
to the side and down the legs.
Smooth the fabric up into the
indentation and down along leg. (Note:
As usual, if glue dries simply apply
more until fabric adheres.)

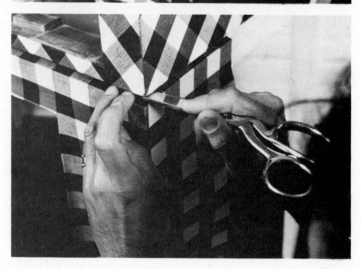

*Illus. 238*
Always make certain that the fabric
is glued well into the indentation. Repeat
steps in illus. 237–238 for other side.

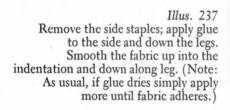

*Illus. 239*
Slit fabric at top and sides of legs.

*Illus. 240*
Cut away excess fabric at bottom of desk between legs.

*Illus. 241*
Apply glue to the inside of the leg. Bring the fabric around from the front and paste it down.

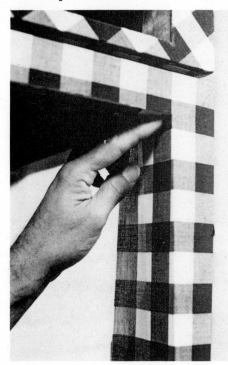

*Illus. 242*
Trim away excess fabric.

*Illus. 243*
Repeat this at the side, making certain to slit tiny flaps at the bottom. Treat the other front leg in the same fashion.

103

*Illus. 244*
Being careful to match the repeats in the fabric, take pieces of fabric long enough to extend along the sides of the desk and one-t of the way on both sides along the back. Repeat the process used for legs and indentation at front on these areas.

*Illus. 245*
Apply glue and seal flaps on all legs.

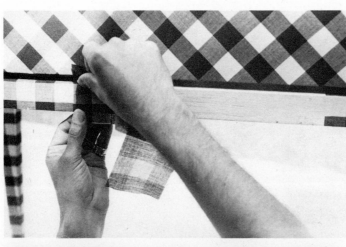

*Illus. 246*
There will be an empty strip in the rear.

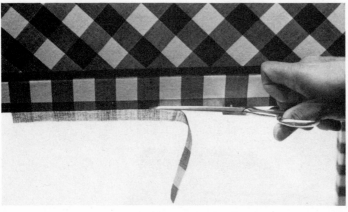

*Illus. 247*
Glue a strip of fabric over it and into the indentation. Make certain that the repeats line up as closely as possible with side strips. Trim excess fabric at bottom.

104

*Illus. 248*
If repeats are properly aligned, patch will be invisible. Check for loose threads. Use glue to stiffen threads and cut them off.

The desk in the gingham room is actually a Grand Rapids adaptation of a campaign desk. Since inexpensive and fairly faithful copies of these Napoleonic desks are now available at several unpainted furniture stores and suppliers, it might be fun to do one in fabric. For the best results, follow these simple instructions:

1. Remove all of the metal fittings.

2. "Fabric-cate" the top and drawer in the same manner as the gingham room desk top.

3. Apply fabric to the legs. If it is possible to disassemble them and treat each one separately, do so.

4. Line the drawer with fabric as in the gingham room desk drawer.

5. Reassemble the desk and replace the hardware.

Following the instructions for lining the gingham room desk drawer (*see* illus. 249–253), one can line the drawers of any piece of furniture, even those to which one does not apply fabric. It can provide a lovely and subtle note, in any room, to open a drawer and find that it has been done in the same material used for the drapes, spreads, or upholstery.

The first step in doing any desk drawer is to remove pulls, knobs, all hardware. If the drawer

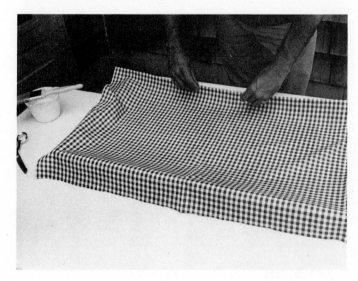

**Lining a Drawer**
*Illus. 249*
Cut a piece of fabric large enough to cover the bottom and sides of the drawer. Apply glue and smooth the material along bottom and sides. Don't worry about bunching at corners.

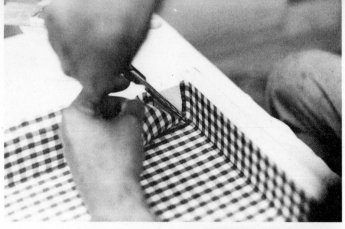

*Illus. 250*
Make slits along the corner
**angles** and remove the
wedge-shaped excess fabric.

*Illus. 251*
Piece the new corner edges
together and glue them snugly
into the angles. Trim away excess
fabric along the top of the drawer.

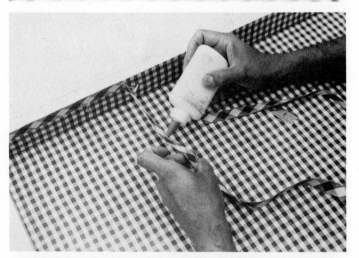

*Illus. 252*
Buy or make ribbon and glue
it along the top of the drawer.
Pin while gluing to help keep
ribbon in place as it dries.

*Illus. 253*
A corner of the lined drawer.

is stained, give it a coat of flat white paint. Plane or sand the edges. Fabric and paint will add a bulk that might make the drawers stick when replaced.

One of Perez's simplest bits of fabric magic was the conversion of an old box spring into the lovely divan in the gingham room (*see* color insert, fig. 22). It was a bit of upholstery that was accomplished without any stitchery. The entire job was done with a staple gun and some staples. (For detailed instructions, *see* illus. 254–268.)

**The Divan**
*Illus. 254*
The box spring.

*Illus. 255*
Cut (or have cut) four small triangles rounded at one point to match the corners of the box spring. Hammer them to the corners. The legs will eventually be screwed into these trianglar shapes.

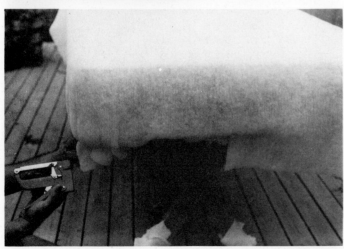

*Illus. 256*
Cut a piece of flannel or batting large enough to completely cover the top and sides of the box spring. Begin stapling the four sides first. Pull the flannel as tautly as possible to prevent wrinkling at the top. Be extremely generous in the use of staples.

107

*Illus. 257*
Do the corners and trim excess fabric.
Notice the slightly shirred effect.

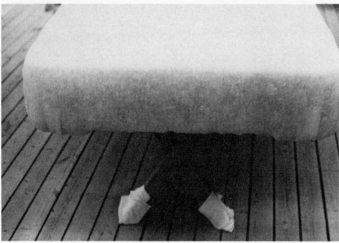

*Illus. 258*
The box spring.

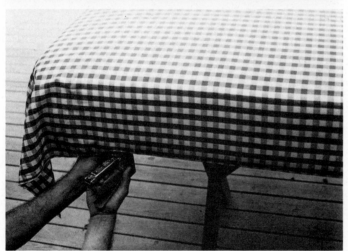

*Illus. 259*
Cut a piece of upholstery fabric (in this
case, gingham) the same size as the
flannel. If it is not available in the
required width, piece together two
lengths of upholstery fabric, making sure
to align the pattern repeats. Cover
the box spring with the fabric exactly as
with the flannel.

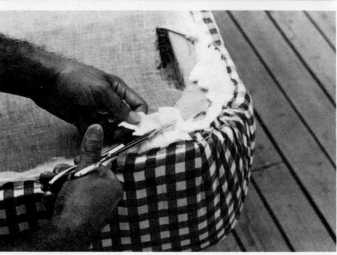

*Illus. 260*
Turn the box spring over and finish
trimming; try to remain as close
as possible to the staples.

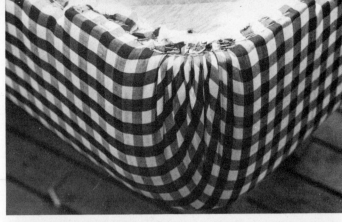

*Illus. 261*
Detail of a corner showing the
generous use of staples.

*Illus. 262*
The completely stapled and
trimmed back.

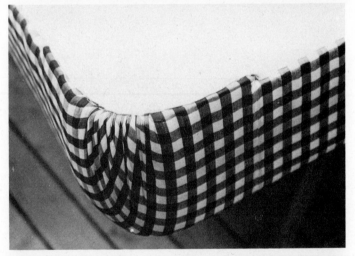

*Illus. 263*
As a finishing touch, a piece of plain
fabric or ticking can be cut
and stapled to the back.

*Illus. 264*
Cut a circle of fabric large enough to
wrap around and cover the
newel-shaped leg. Make a series of slits
around the circumference of the
fabric to within an inch of the
center of the circle.

*Illus. 265*
Screw the leg into a piece of wood; apply glue to the leg and press the fabric as tightly as possible over it. Make certain that none of the wood shows through.

*Illus. 266*
The glued and wrapped leg.

*Illus. 267*
Glue and staple the fabric around the bottom of the leg. Treat the other legs in the same fashion. Screw them into the triangles at the four corners of the box spring.

*Illus. 268*
A mattress can be added to convert the box spring into a bed. (*See* color insert, fig. 22.)

The result can serve as a comfortable low divan, piled high with pillows, as in the gingham room; topped with a mattress, it becomes a bed that needs no dust ruffles or headboard to make it a decorative asset in any guest room.

One of the most satisfying things about this piece is the economy with which it is created. The spring can be one that's been stored in the attic for years or one that's been picked up for a few dollars at a thrift shop or secondhand furniture store. The legs are the tops of newels, available at almost any lumber yard. The fabric can be one of those colorful sheets that are being created by such leading designers as Bill Blass and Yves St. Laurent. The tuck-under will provide the necessary fabric for covering the legs.

A contour sheet might provide a shortcut, but it will not eliminate the necessity for pulling the material tautly, nor will it circumvent the abundant use of staples. In this instance, an extra pillow case will supply the fabric for the legs.

If covering all the other furniture in the room was undergraduate work, the armchair represented a postgraduate course (*see* color insert, fig. 23). Until now, this fantasy of fabric and color could only have been executed by Luis Perez. It is a supreme example of the conversion of a prosaic, machine-made piece of furniture into something of such brilliance that interior designers who have already seen it have observed, "It belongs in the Museum of Decorative Arts."

Using the guidelines for the handling of fabric, covering a similar chair should not prove too difficult.

Excluding cording and ribbon, forty-three individual pieces of gingham were pasted directly onto the wooden frame of the chair; thirty additional pieces were used to make the patchwork fabric on the seat.

The design is an intricate balance of bias-cut and regular-cut pieces. That this most complex and difficult piece should remain his favorite is indicative both of Perez's dedication to his craft and the pleasure he derives from its successful execution. (Illus. 269–299 depict the various steps that went into the "fabric-cation" of the gingham armchair.)

**The Armchair**
*Illus.* 269
The chair as it appeared before the seat fabric was removed and the wood was painted white.

*Illus.* 270
To cover the spoke in the backrest, cut a piece of fabric on the bias slightly longer and wider than the spoke.

111

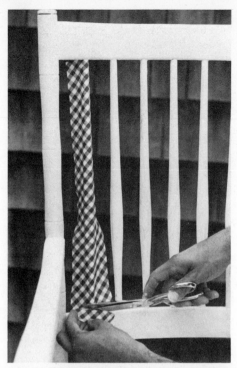

*Illus. 271*
Glue it to the front; trim the excess length
of fabric right on the chair to make certain that
no error in measuring has occurred. Continue
to glue the piece of fabric around the spoke.

*Illus. 273*
Cut a strip of fabric on the bias wide enough
to wrap around the armrest and long
enough to reach under the handrest.
Glue it down.

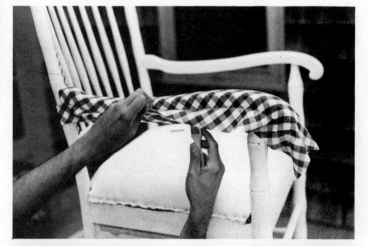

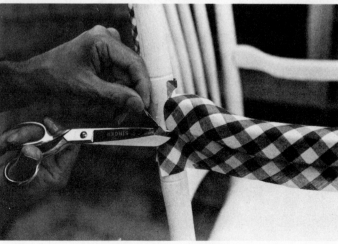

*Illus. 272*
Trim the excess fabric at the seam.
If there is a ridge of fabric or overlapping,
run a razor blade along the seam,
reach in with a pin, and pull out
the excess strip from underneath.

*Illus. 274*
Trim the excess fabric at the rear
of the armrest. Use both scissors and
blade for delicate work.

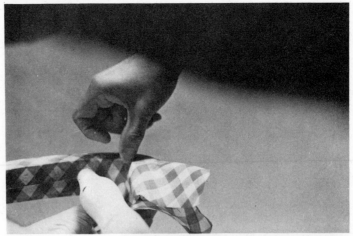

*Illus. 275*
Trim and glue around the front leg.

*Illus. 277*
Glue the top flap down and under; be sure to glue thoroughly; then trim.

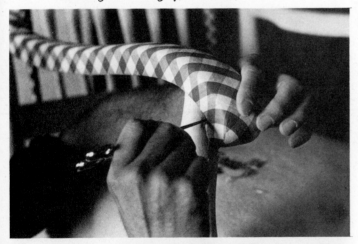

*Illus. 276*
Make two cuts to the start of the handrest. Glue the side flaps down.

*Illus. 278*
Make slits around sides with razor blade.

113

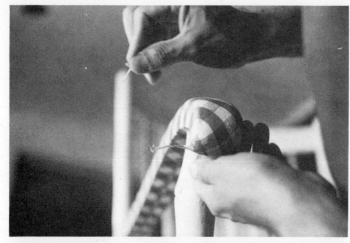

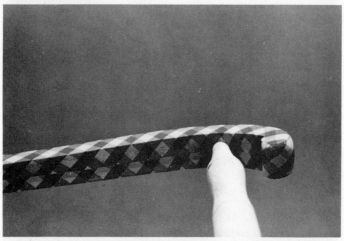

*Illus. 279*
Reach under with pin to remove
excess fabric.

*Illus. 280*
The finished armrest.

*Illus. 281*
A portion of the mock-bamboo back
frame; note that each section is
individually covered in fabric.

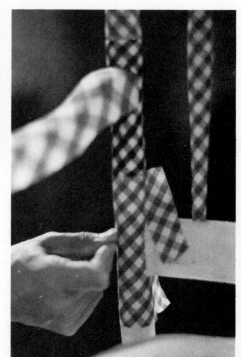

*Illus. 282*
The cutting and fitting of fabric
around one of the crossbars.

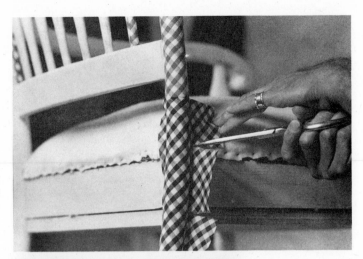

*Illus. 283*
The fabric for the leg is cut,
fitted, and glued at seat-level.

*Illus. 284*
Glue the fabric to the section of the front
leg immediately under the armrest.

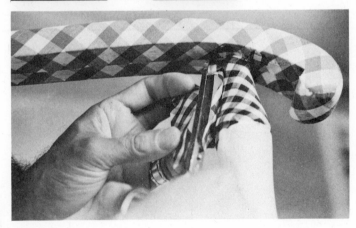

*Illus. 285*
Trim the excess fabric.

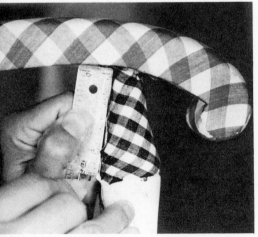

*Illus. 286*
Make a cut with a razor blade along
the seam.

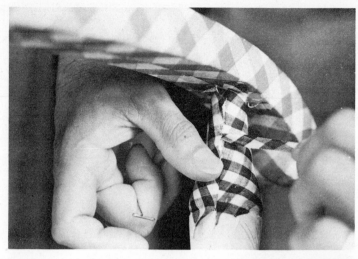

*Illus.* 287
Use a pin to pull out excess fabric
from underneath.

*Illus.* 288
Make slits to fit fabric around spokes.

*Illus.* 289
The fabric is glued down and trimmed.

*Illus.* 290
For patchwork seat fabric, cut a 2¾″ (the
¾″ is for seam) square cardboard model.
Trace the shape on several gingham
fabrics of different size checks.

*Illus. 291*
Cut out the squares and
stitch them together.

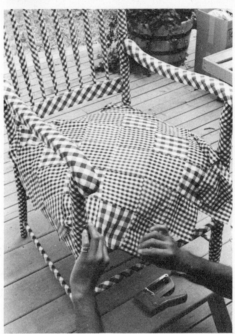

*Illus. 292*
When sufficient patchwork is made to
cover the seat, lay it aside. Staple a flannel
lining to seat and trim. Then staple the
patchwork over the flannel.

*Illus. 294*
A detail of the stapling at the leg.

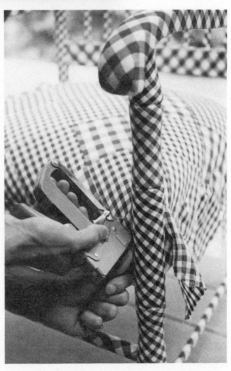

*Illus. 293*
Make a slit to fit fabric around leg. The
fabric is pulled tautly and stapled to seat.

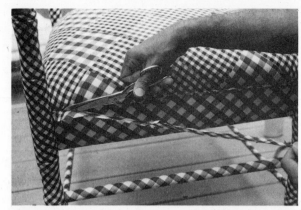

*Illus. 295*
Excess fabric is trimmed beneath the staple line.

*Illus. 296*
To conceal the staples, ribbon is made (*see* steps in illus. 32–36) and paste is applied to one side; it is then glued over the staples.

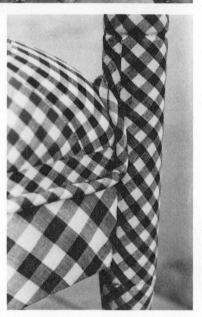

*Illus. 298*
A detail showing the seams of one of the legs.

*Illus. 297*
Cording is made (*see* steps in illus. 39–42) and pasted around the entire seat.

*Illus. 299*
A detail of the top of the chair.

118

Nothing is sacred to a first-rate fabric-crafter. That includes the machines of this industrial age. He does not believe in the inviolateness of their pristine sterility. After all, these machines are generally the products of other machines in a chain of automated spontaneous generation. Hand-crafting helps to give them some degree of individuality.

If the opportunity could be found, Luis Perez would probably lend the warmth of a homey living room to an icily forbidding IBM computer by covering it in glazed cotton. In the gingham room, he believed that the television and telephone had to conform to his rule that everything be covered in gingham. They were neither fine porcelain nor delicately-wrought *objets d'art*; they were things that most people hide away. A little fabric turned them into novel conversation pieces that added handsomely to the décor (*see* color insert, figs. 24 and 25).

Covering these implements is not difficult. All it takes is patience and a delicacy of touch and cutting. Fabric, glue, scissors, and razor blades are the only items necessary to do the job. (For detailed instructions on covering a telephone, *see* illus. 300–325; for the television set, *see* illus. 326–345.)

### The Telephone

*Illus. 300*
The telephone in its original state. (Note: Always work with a privately purchased phone.) It is best to use a white phone; if purchased in a color other than white, the phone must be painted white.

*Illus. 301*
Being careful to avoid the dial and carriage, apply glue with a brush to the front of the phone and between the carriage.

119

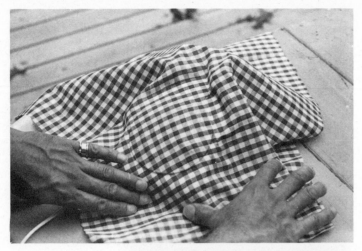

Illus. 302
Cut a rectangle of fabric large enough to easily enshroud phone. (Note: Do not use fabric which is too stiff or too heavy.) Smooth it down over the glue-coated area. Apply more glue if it dries before fabric is completely pasted down.

Illus. 303
Using a razor blade, carefully free the two front carriage prongs and the dial.

Illus. 304
Cut around the two carriage sections. Glue the center portion down.

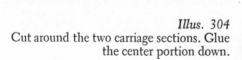

Illus. 305
Lift the fabric and apply glue to the sides of the phone. Smooth the fabric down, being careful to press the fabric into all curved areas so that no wrinkles or bubbles appear.

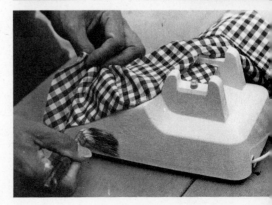

120

*Illus. 306*
Make a slit in the fabric to free the wire.

*Illus. 307*
Slit fabric at rear of phone down the center.
Trim away part of the excess fabric from
one half of the rear of phone, leaving enough on
the other half to cover the entire rear surface.

*Illus. 308*
Smooth fabric across the rear area, trimming
around carriage and pushing into hollow
area as much as possible.

*Illus. 309*
Cut a separate rectangle large
enough to cover
the hollow area under the carriage.

121

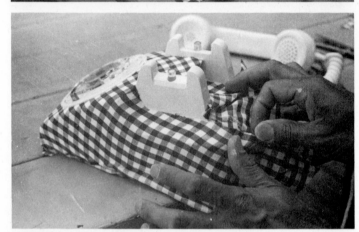

*Illus. 310*
Apply glue to hollow area and poke rectangle into all sides.

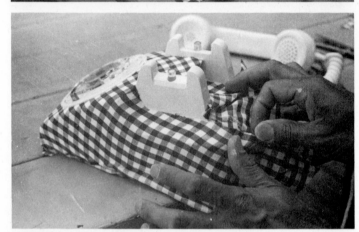

*Illus. 311*
Using scissors, razor blade, and fingers, smooth and trim seam area at rear corner of phone.

*Illus. 312*
Trim fabric at bottom of phone. Apply glue to crevice around casing and use scissors to push fabric up into it.

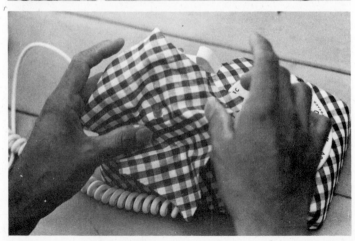

*Illus. 313*
Cut hole in center of small piece of fabric. Apply glue to carriage section. Place hole over button; glue and smooth fabric down.

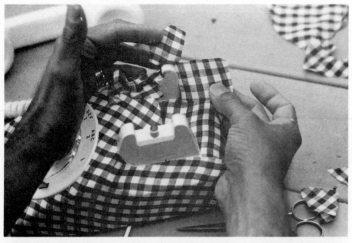

*Illus. 314*
Cut slits at carriage peaks to
facilitate wrapping procedure.

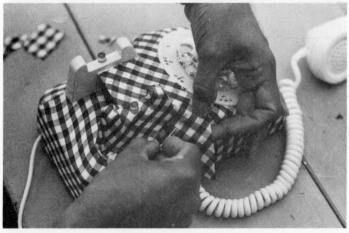

*Illus. 315*
Continue smoothing out fabric,
adding glue, and then trimming.

*Illus. 316*
Carefully cut away excess fabric
at one side with razor blade
so that design blends into
previously applied fabric.

*Illus. 317*
One completed side. Repeat for
other side. Do not forget to push
fabric into hollow area.

123

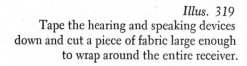

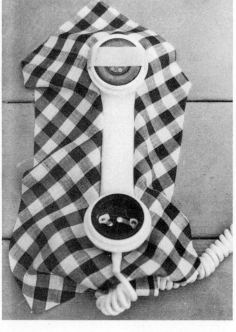

*Illus. 318*
Unscrew caps at each end of receiver.

*Illus. 319*
Tape the hearing and speaking devices down and cut a piece of fabric large enough to wrap around the entire receiver.

*Illus. 320*
Apply glue to top of receiver and wrap fabric firmly around it so that no wrinkles appear.

*Illus. 321*
Trim excess fabric and cut slits on both sides of each end of the handle. Glue and seal fabric around it.

124

*Illus.* 322
Trim excess fabric and cut slits at ends of hearing and speaking mechanisms.

*Illus.* 323
Glue slitted fabric around back of hearing and speaking mechanisms and trim.

*Illus.* 324
Glue narrow strips of fabric around detached caps of speaking and hearing devices. Trim and rescrew caps in place.

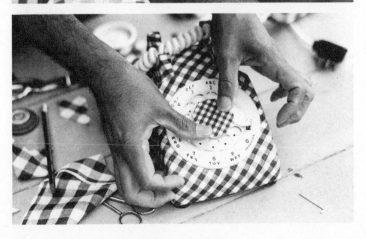

*Illus.* 325
To add a finishing touch, glue a small circle of fabric over the center of the dial.

### The Television Set
*Illus.* 326
Remove the knobs. Tape some strips of paper around screen to protect it. Paint the set white. (Its appearance should already seem improved.)

*Illus.* 327
Glue a strip of fabric along the top of the screen. Miter corners and trim around screen with razor blade, being especially careful not to scratch it.

*Illus.* 328
Repeat this process for both sides of set, always smoothing fabric out and tucking it into ridges to prevent wrinkling.

*Illus.* 329
Make certain fabric is securely glued to three sides of set before trimming excess fabric.

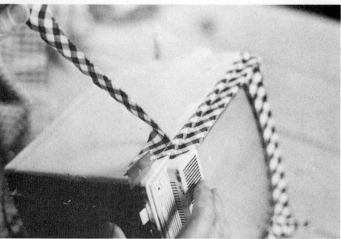

126

*Illus. 330*
Glue and smooth a piece of
fabric from bottom of screen to
bottom of set. Make hole to fit
over prongs for knobs so that
fabric will lay flat.

*Illus. 331*
Cut around channel selector
and major controls.

*Illus. 332*
Make slits to free the speaker.

*Illus. 333*
Cut a rectangle of fabric large
enough so that it can be draped
over the top and down the
sides of the set. Glue down top
portion from handle to the front.
Make diagonal cuts from far
corners to handle.

127

*Illus. 334*
Slip the fabric through the handle.

*Illus. 335*
Glue and smooth down rest of
fabric for top, carefully piecing
fabric around handle. Trim
threads and bits of fabric
resulting from piecing.

*Illus. 336*
Make slit from diagonal cut
to antenna.

*Illus. 337*
While piecing together diagonal
cuts, start gluing down the side.
If there is a tuner, cut a flap over
it before completing the
gluing operation.

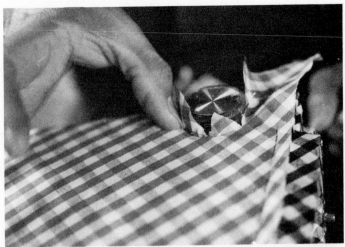

*Illus. 338*
Cut slits; glue and piece the flap around the tuner. Trim excess fabric and complete gluing operation.

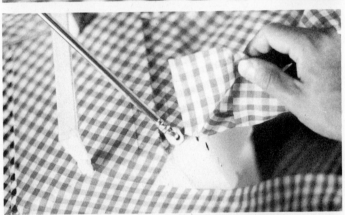

*Illus. 339*
Finish covering and gluing side by piecing fabric behind antenna to diagonal slit. There should be suffcent fabric remaining to match the squares.

*Illus. 340*
Detail of antenna section after completion of piecing and gluing operation.

*Illus. 341*
Make slits at rear corners of set.

*Illus. 342*
Piece fabric together, glue, smooth it
into ridges, and trim.

*Illus. 343*
View of bottom of set (after trimming
with scissors and razor blade).

*Illus. 344*
Cover edges of set with cording and ribbon.
Because of the fragility of the fabric strips
across the speaker, it might be wiser to
completely free the speaker and touch it up
with paint.

*Illus. 345*
Detail of controls after knobs have been
replaced. Notice cording around screen.

130

# "Fabric-cated" Objects

AN ASTONISHING ARRAY of small objects can be covered with fabric to heighten their decorative interest and enhance their looks. For covering objects, again, the only tools necessary are glue, sharp scissors, and razor blades.

There are a variety of things that can easily be covered with fabric: frames, clocks, wastepaper baskets, boxes, trays, vases, lamps, and flowerpots.

A coat of flat white paint is the first step in working with any of them. This will prevent the original color or metal from showing through and discoloring the material that is to cover them.

Soft, pliable fabrics such as cottons are the best bets when working on these limited surfaces. Never use a permanent press material for the reason already given—it does not fold easily into corners and angles.

To cover the picture frame (*see* illus. 346), Luis took it apart and covered one side at a time (*see* illus. 347). Other picture frames with different kinds of moldings can also be handsomely "fabric-cated" (*see* illus. 348). To "fabric-cate" the frame of a rectangular mirror, *see* illus. 349–356.

*Illus. 347*

## The Mirror
*Illus. 349*
The mirror as it appears before a coat of flat white paint has been applied to the frame.

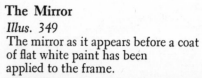

*Illus. 350*
The mirror will require three strips of variously patterned gingham for each side. The molding will be cut free at the corners. Glue a strip of fabric to each of the four outer edges of the mirror. Press it firmly into all indentations.

*Illus. 351*
After the glue has dried, carefully cut around the molding with a razor blade.

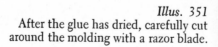

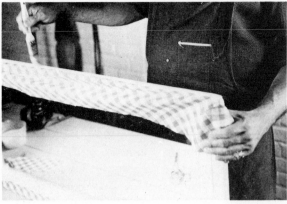

*Illus. 352*
Glue the fabric to the rear of the mirror.

*Illus. 353*
The exposed outer molding after trimming with razor blade.

*Illus. 354*
Glue strips of fabric over the four sides of the inner part of the frame (the ridge is the dividing line). Start freeing the molding with razor blade.

*Illus. 355*
The freed molding. A section of the inner frame which has been cut away to make room for the final strip. Each of these four inner strips are glued to the corresponding edges of the mirror. Since there is no molding, no particular care in cutting is required.

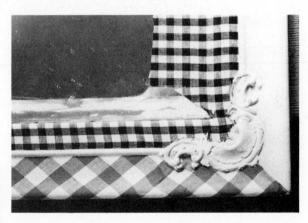

*Illus. 356*
The completed mirror. A more lavish way to "fabric-cate" a mirror or frame is to completely cover it with a piece of fabric and then cut out the center. This alternative procedure involves three successive operations. After all the sections are glued in place, the outlines of the moldings are found and subsequently cut free. This method does not require much more work, and its final effect is infinitely superior to the first method.

133

A combination of ricrac and gingham can be combined to make a charming vase (see illus. 357). A straw sewing basket can be given a delicate finish with a fabric lid (see illus. 358); ribbon of the same fabric can be woven into the straw (see illus. 359); it can also be used to line the interior. (See illus. 360; note that the fabric in this latter illustration is a printed patchwork design and not a handmade patchwork.)

*Illus. 357*

*Illus. 358*

*Illus. 359*

*Illus. 360*

Lovely things can be done to little unpainted boxes (*see* illus. 361 and 362) and chests (*see* illus. 363). One can have fun by using two fab- rics on one piece, by centering a printed motif, or by just doing the job well.

For the gingham room, Luis covered a flower-

*Illus. 361*

*Illus. 362*

*Illus. 363*

pot, a wastepaper basket, a lamp plus shade, and a clock. (For lamp and shade, *see* illus. 364–379; for clock, *see* illus. 380–394; for flowerpot, *see* illus. 395–402; for wastepaper basket, *see* illus. 403–407.) As one can see from the instruction photographs, the process is not a difficult one, nor does it take long to do. A flowerpot or wastepaper basket can be finished in less than half an hour (after the base coat of white paint has dried).

### The Desk Lamp and Shade
*Illus. 364*
The lamp, a Woolworth's item.

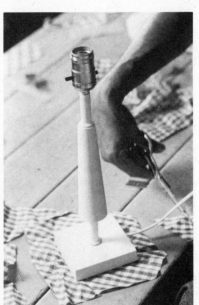

*Illus. 365*
After painting the base of the lamp white, cut a piece of fabric large enough to wrap around the base.

*Illus. 366*
Coat the base with glue. Make a slit reaching to the center of the fabric. Slide the fabric over the base, making sure that the slit is directly over the wire. Smooth the fabric down.

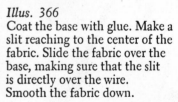

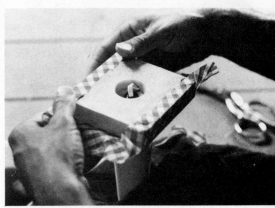

*Illus. 367*
Paste two (opposite) ends of the fabric over to back of base.

136

*Illus.* 368
Make slits at all four corners.

*Illus.* 369
Make a horizontal cut just beneath
wire, thus forming a flap. Trim around
wire; glue flap closed under wire so
that fabric lays smoothly around it.

*Illus.* 370
Glue remaining two sides around to
back of base and trim excess fabric
at corners.

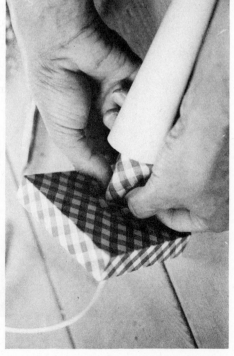

*Illus.* 371
Cut, glue, smooth, and trim a piece of
fabric around the next upper
section of lamp.

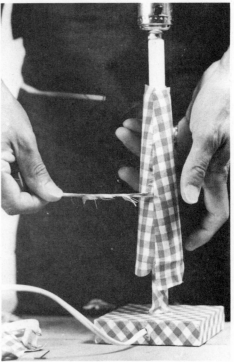

*Illus.* 372
Continue in same fashion for all sections of lamp.

*Illus.* 373
Cut through outer and inner layers of fabric at seam and pull out excess strips. This will eliminate ridge. Then glue. At points where wider sections meet narrower ones, feather the edge with slit; this will make it easier to glue them down. Continue until lamp shaft has been completely "fabric-cated."

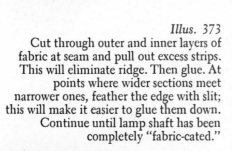

## The Shade

*Illus.* 374
Cut a piece of fabric a little wider and longer than the circumference of the shade. Smooth fabric and glue it down over shade.

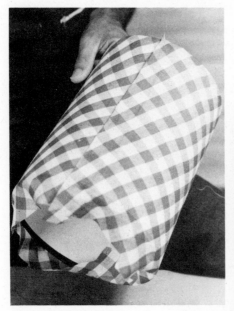

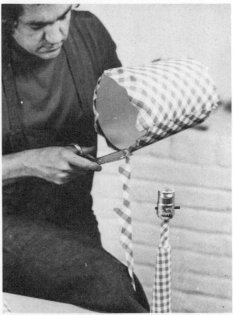

138

*Illus.* 375
Trim to within ½" of both top and bottom.

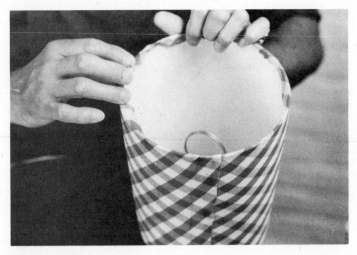

*Illus. 376*
Tuck small flaps into top and
bottom of shade and paste down.

*Illus. 377*
At bottom, decorate exterior of
shade with a band or ribbon. Use
a second band to hold the flaps
securely on the inside.

*Illus. 378*
Trim the top with ribbon
and cording.

*Illus. 379*
The completed lamp.

139

## The Clock

*Illus. 380*
The clock, an item purchased in a second-hand store.

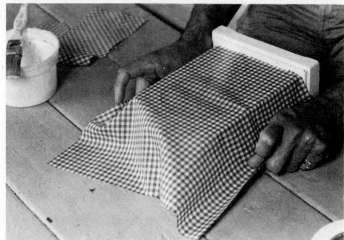

*Illus. 381*
Remove clock mechanism and paint the case white. Cut a piece of fabric large enough to cover the whole clock (excluding the pedestal) and stretch it around to rear. Glue it to the front (face) side.

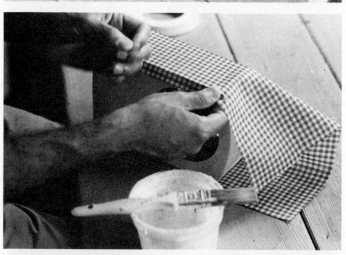

*Illus. 382*
Glue the fabric to the sides of the clock and around the back.

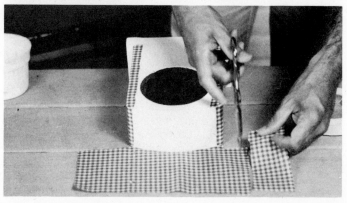

*Illus. 383*
Make slits at the upper portion of the sides and cut some of the excess fabric away.

140

*Illus. 384*
Glue the top down and over
to the rear.

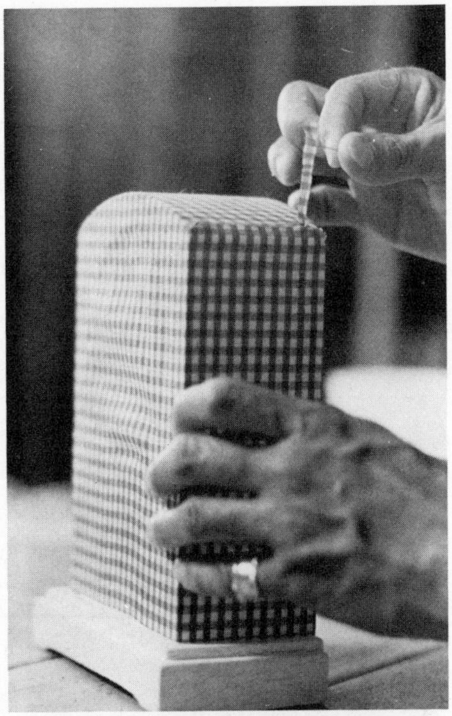

*Illus. 385*
Use scissors and razor blade to trim excess
fabric where top and sides meet. After making
a corner razor cut, pull out the extra strip of
fabric from underneath. Use more glue to
seal the corner.

*Illus. 386*
The sealed seam.

*Illus. 387*
Run razor blade around perimeter of front
face opening to remove excess fabric.

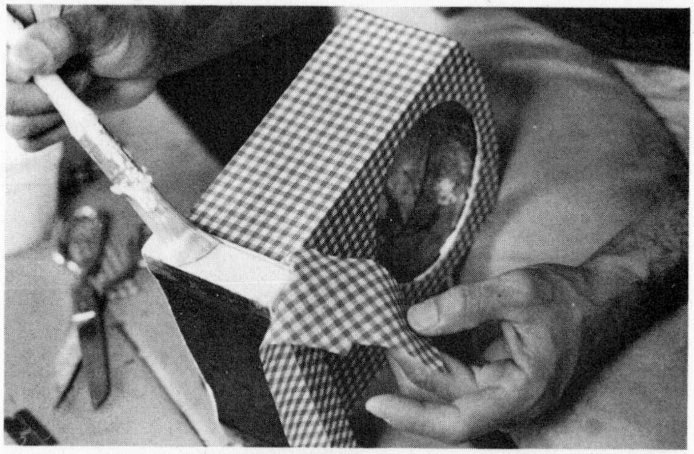

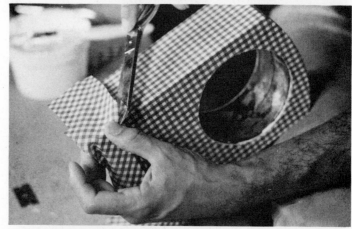

*Illus. 388*
Glue a strip of fabric around
front and sides of the pedestal.

*Illus. 389*
A slit is made at the corners; glue
is applied to the ridges.

*Illus. 390*
A sharp instrument is used to push
the fabric into the ridges so
that it meets the previously glued
fabric for the upper portion
of the clock.

*Illus. 391*
Fabric is glued in position on the
sides. Excess fabric is trimmed
away. A little lip of fabric is glued
to bottom of pedestal.

142

*Illus.* 392
A piece of fabric is cut, glued, and trimmed on the rear side of clock. A hole is cut for the rear face.

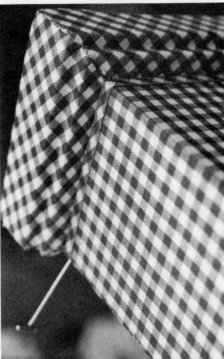

*Illus.* 393
Use ribbon to trim the pedestal. Pins will hold ribbon in place while drying.

*Illus.* 394
The mechanism is replaced. A piece of felt is cut, pasted, and trimmed to the bottom of the clock.

143

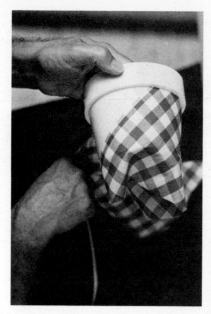

## The Flowerpot
*Illus. 395*
Cut a piece of fabric slightly longer and wider than the area beneath the lip of the pot. (In this case, cut on the bias.) Start gluing the fabric around the pot.

*Illus. 396*
Because the pot angles in at the base, the fabric must be pulled very tautly and smoothed out with care. If necessary, add glue as you go.

*Illus. 398*
Trim excess fabric from bottom of pot.

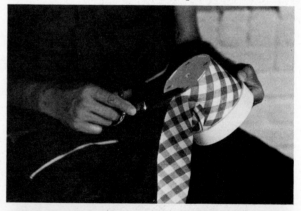

*Illus. 397*
Cut excess fabric (on bias) as close to starting point as possible. There should be little or no ridge.

*Illus. 399*
Cut a strip of fabric (not as bias) long enough to encircle the lip. Glue it down.

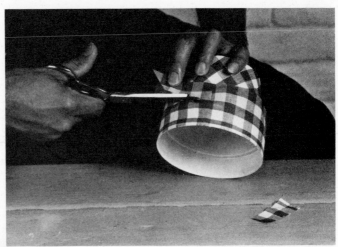

*Illus. 400*
Trim very close to (but not at the edge of) the bottom of the lip.

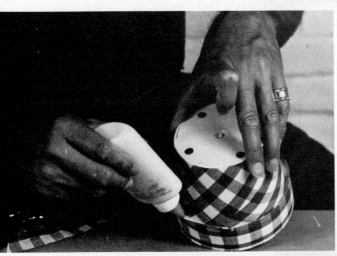

*Illus. 401*
Apply a fine stream of glue along bottom of lip and fold fabric up and in, carefully pressing it to insides of lip.

*Illus. 402*
The finished pot. For flowerpots in which plants are to be placed, shellac and varnish the "fabric-cated" pot so that water will not harm them.

## The Wastepaper Basket

*Illus. 403*
The finished basket. The body was glued exactly as it was for the flowerpot.

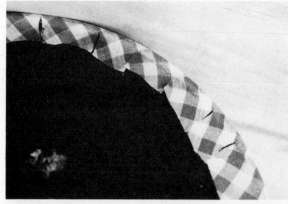

*Illus. 404*
Instead of trimming precisely at bottom edge, leave fabric 1″ longer, feather with slits, and glue up under basket. The bottom can be finished off with a disk of felt pasted over the edges of the fabric.

*Illus. 405*
For the top, cut the fabric a little more than 1″ above the height of the basket and paste down along the inside. This is then masked with a wide band of ribbon pasted along the top edge of the basket.

*Illus. 406*
Baskets can be decorated with several rows of variously patterned ribbon pasted over each other.

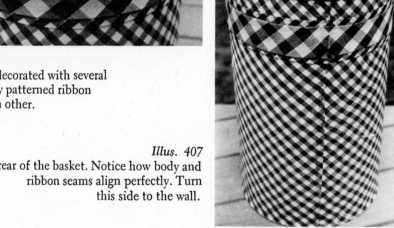

*Illus. 407*
The rear of the basket. Notice how body and ribbon seams align perfectly. Turn this side to the wall.

Once you begin to see rooms and furnishings from a "fabric-cating" point of view, you begin to see ways of renewing the life of all manner of discards. You can also find 1,001 ways to save money by redoing and creating things that are far more individually yours and visually exciting than those for which large sums are paid in shops—and doing this inexpensively in your spare time. Luis Perez has proven that fabric is fun. Certainly, doing everything in fabric may be extreme, but doing some things in fabric is always a visual pleasure.